The Ekklesia
The Kingdom Embassy in the Earth

Christopher Turney

Scripture Credits

Unless otherwise noted, all Scripture quotations are taken from the New King James Version® (NKJV).

Copyright © 1982 by Thomas Nelson. Used by permission. All rights reserved.

Scripture quotations marked AMP are taken from the Amplified Bible,

Copyright © 1954, 1958, 1962, 1964, 1965, 1987 by The Lockman Foundation. Used by permission.

(www.Lockman.org)

Scripture quotations marked KJV are taken from the King James Version of the Bible.

Public Domain.

Scripture quotations marked NIV are taken from the Holy Bible, New International Version®, NIV®.

Copyright © 1973, 1978, 1984, 2011 by Biblica, Inc.™ Used by permission.

All rights reserved worldwide.

Scripture quotations marked ESV are from The Holy Bible, English Standard Version® (ESV®),

Copyright © 2001 by Crossway, a publishing ministry of Good News Publishers. Used by permission.

All rights reserved.

Scripture quotations marked NASB are from the New American Standard Bible®, NASB®.

Copyright © 1960, 1962, 1963, 1968, 1971, 1972, 1973, 1975, 1977, 1995, 2020 by The Lockman Foundation.

(www.Lockman.org). Used by permission. All rights reserved.

Scripture quotations marked NLT are from the Holy Bible, New Living Translation,

Copyright © 1996, 2004, 2015 by Tyndale House Foundation. Used by permission of Tyndale House Publishers, Carol Stream, Illinois 60188. All rights reserved.

Copyright Page

Ekklesia: The Kingdom Embassy in the Earth

© 2025 Christopher K. Turney

All rights reserved.

No part of this publication may be reproduced, stored in a retrieval system, or transmitted in any form or by any means—electronic, mechanical, photocopying, recording, or otherwise—without the prior written permission of the publisher, except in the case of brief quotations embodied in critical articles or reviews.

All rights reserved worldwide.

ISBN: 979-8-218-94131-4

Printed in the United States of America.

For information, visit: www.chrisandjillturney.com

Table of Contents

Acknowledgments vii

Foreword ix

Preface xi

Introduction xiii

Chapter 1 His Church 15
Chapter 2 The Ekklesia He Spoke Of 23
Chapter 3 The Revelation That Builds And Binds 31
Chapter 4 Lively Stones Or Man-Made Bricks? 41
Chapter 5 The Government Of The Kingdom 53
Chapter 6 Embassies Of Heaven In The Earth 61
Chapter 7 The Culture Of The Kingdom 71
Chapter 8 The Call To Discipleship 79
Chapter 9 Sonship, The Maturity Of The House 87
Chapter 10 Jointly Fit, The Architecture Of The Body 95
Chapter 11 The Glory In The House, The Objective 103
Chapter 12 The Prophetic Blueprint Building According To Heaven's Pattern 111
Chapter 13 The Order Of Establishment Reclaiming Divine Chronology 119
Chapter 14 The Invisible Foundation, The Unseen Necessity Of Apostles And Prophets 127
Chapter 15 The Sound Of The House, Presence, Alignment, And Governmental Worship 133
Chapter 16 Legacy And Generations Building Beyond Our Day 139
Chapter 17 Not A Community Church 145

About The Author 151

Acknowledgments

I want to express my heartfelt gratitude to those who have stood with me in life and in purpose. Every stone in this journey has been laid with love, prayer, and partnership.

To my wife, Jill, your steadfast love, strength, and grace have been a constant reminder of the Father's heart. You have walked beside me through every season, and your faith has anchored our home in peace and purpose.

To my mother, whose unyielding faith and prayers formed the foundation of who I am, and to my stepfather, Ron, whose steady hand, integrity, and quiet strength helped shape my life, thank you both for embodying the values this book proclaims: faith, perseverance, and love that builds.

To my children, you are my living legacy. Each of you carries a piece of my heart and a reflection of the Kingdom. Being your father is one of my greatest honors in this life. I love you more than words can express.

To Bishop Gary and Pastor Lydia Clowers, your spiritual parenting, example, and covering continue to guide my steps. Thank you for believing in me and for helping me build what Heaven has designed.

To the Kingdom Reign Ministries family, you are not just a congregation, you are a family. You are living stones, joined together by revelation and love, building something that represents Heaven on earth. Thank you for your faith, your labor, and your devotion to the vision.

To every leader, son, daughter, and co-laborer in this Kingdom movement, this book is for you. May it call forth the builder within you, the reformer in you, and the worshiper who builds according to Heaven's pattern.

And to my Abba Father, the Master Builder of all, thank You for allowing me to take part in what You are constructing in the earth. May this book glorify You and help raise a people who build Your Ekklesia according to divine design.

Foreword

There are moments in history when Heaven issues a call so clear that it pierces through the noise of religion, routine, and ritual. This book is one of those moments. It is a clarion call, a trumpet sound to the Body of Christ to remember who we are and why we were placed in the earth. What Apostle Christopher Turney has written is not merely a book; it is a prophetic disruption.

The word Ekklesia was never meant to describe a Sunday gathering or a community center. Ekklesia is not a building, a brand, or a calendar of services. It was Heaven's governmental design for transformation, alignment, and dominion. History tells the story of how costly this truth has been to protect. In 1522, William Tyndale dared to translate Ekklesia in Matthew 16:18 as congregation rather than church, reflecting its true intent as a called-out governing assembly. For this act of obedience, he was condemned and later executed in 1536 for refusing to recant. In many ways, this book serves as a restoration of that truth, a righting of what was once lost.

Through these pages, Apostle Turney dismantles the systems that have confined the Church to programs and performance, calling her instead to return to revelation, presence, and power. Each chapter builds like a blueprint, revealing the architecture of Heaven's design, the order of divine government, and the necessity of alignment between apostles, prophets, and the people of God. He exposes the danger of building without revelation and reveals the beauty of a Church that governs rather than merely gathers.

CHRISTOPHER TURNEY

Apostle Turney's words confront complacency, expose imitation, and reignite a holy conviction, a deep, unshakable certainty of who we are and what we are called to build. They call the Church to move beyond comfort and step boldly into Kingdom function, to become again the vibrant, governing Ekklesia that shakes regions and establishes Heaven's rule in the earth.

As you read, prepare to be unsettled in the best possible way. Expect your definitions to be challenged, your spirit to be stirred, and your understanding of "church" to be radically expanded. This book does not flatter the reader; it commissions them. It calls forth the builder in you, the son in you, the reformer in you. You will not finish these pages the same way you began them, because the revelation within was never meant to leave the reader unchanged. This is a blueprint for the brave, a guide for those who dare to partner with Heaven's architecture in this hour of divine reconstruction.

May your heart burn as you read.
May your spirit awaken as truth confronts tradition.

And may you, like the early apostles, rise as part of the Ekklesia that turns the world upside down once again.

Dr. Tony Robinson
CEO & Founder, Dr. Tony Robinson Consulting

Preface

The Burden Behind the Book

I did not set out to write another book on church growth, ministry models, or leadership strategy. This is not that book. What you hold in your hands is the product of a deep burden, born from years of watching the Church increasingly reflect something other than the nature of Christ.

We have substituted presentation for representation, and as a result, the image of Jesus has been obscured behind lights, platforms, personalities, and productions. The modern church is too often shaped by emotional hype rather than holy presence, by inspiration without impartation, and by service that never becomes sonship.

I have witnessed the rise of ministry performances, well-executed and highly attended, yet spiritually shallow. The atmospheres feel charged, but the fruit is fleeting. What was meant to form disciples has been replaced by a desire to fill rooms. We have mistaken movement for maturity.

This book is my response to that ache. It is a call back to the Ekklesia, not the church we are building, but the one He is. It is a Kingdom summons to see His design restored in the earth: sons and daughters raised, not just volunteers recruited; presence prioritized over performance; and a people who govern in the Spirit, not merely gather in a room.

If you've felt the tension, between what we've made church and what Jesus meant, I invite you to walk this journey with me.

Introduction

From Church as We Know it to Ekklesia as He Designed It

Jesus never said, "I will build My ministry."

He didn't say, "I will build My brand."

He said, *"I will build My Church"* - My Ekklesia (Matthew 16:18).

That single statement reveals both ownership and intention. The Church doesn't belong to us; it belongs to Him. And what He is building is not based on our creativity, preferences, or charisma, it is built upon **revelation**, **identity**, and **authority**.

The Greek word ekklesia was not a religious term. It was a governmental word used in Roman and Greek culture to describe a called-out assembly of citizens summoned to legislate, govern, and represent the authority of a kingdom. Jesus intentionally used this word to describe the kind of people He was forming, those who would not just attend services but advance His Kingdom in the earth.

The modern Church, however, has often drifted far from that original blueprint. We have built services but not sent ones. We've multiplied audiences but not raised ambassadors. What was meant to be a Kingdom embassy, a living, breathing expression of heaven on earth, has been reduced in many places to a religious event, a corporate enterprise, or a motivational platform.

This book is a prophetic call back to the foundation.

It is not a book of critique but of correction. It is not written in cynicism, but in covenant. The Lord is not abandoning His Church, He is refining her. And He is inviting us to return to the Master Builder's plan, to once again become His ekklesia, an embassy of His Kingdom on earth, marked not by style or strategy but by glory, grace, and government.

Throughout these pages, we will explore:

- The difference between the Church we are building and the Church He is building
- The original design and function of the Ekklesia
- How house churches and larger gatherings both had a place in the early Church
- Why revelation is the foundation, and how the gates of Hades (the unseen realm) cannot prevail against it
- What it means to raise sons and daughters, not just members and workers
- How to break the cycle of performance and rediscover the power of presence

This is more than ecclesiology. It is a Kingdom restoration project.

We are not called to imitate the early Church; we are called to fulfill what they began. And to do that, we must recover the identity, structure, and purpose of the Church Jesus is building, the Ekklesia: His Kingdom Embassy in the earth.

CHAPTER 1
HIS CHURCH

"Unless the Lord builds the house, they labor in vain who build it." Psalm 127:1

Jesus said plainly:

"I will build My Church, and the gates of Hades shall not prevail against it."
Matthew 16:18 (NKJV)

This is more than a foundational verse; it is a defining Kingdom decree. In a single sentence, Jesus made three realities clear:

1. He is the builder.
2. The Church (ekklesia) belongs to Him.
3. Hell has no power over what He builds.

But we must ask: Are we agreeing with what He is building?

Or have we, like Israel in the wilderness, erected golden calves and called them YHWH?

The Churches We Build vs. the Church He Builds

There is a vast difference between the churches we are building and the Church He is building. What we often call "church" today may be a system, a service, a structure, or a brand, but not necessarily a revelation-based body formed by the Spirit of Christ.

- Man builds with strategy; Jesus builds with revelation.

- Man builds based on demographics; Jesus builds based on divine DNA.
- Man builds to gather people; Jesus builds to govern territories.
- Man builds for the crowd; Jesus builds for the King.

Psalm 127:1 warns us:

"Unless the Lord builds the house, they labor in vain who build it."

It is possible to be busy building something that Heaven didn't authorize. Activity does not equal alignment. Just because it grows doesn't mean it's God. Just because it works doesn't mean it's Kingdom.

The Revelation Foundation

Jesus asked His disciples, *"Who do you say that I am?"*

Peter answered by revelation:

"You are the Christ, the Son of the Living God."
Jesus responded, "Flesh and blood has not revealed this to you… and upon this rock I will build My Church." (Matt. 16:17–18)

The rock was not Peter, it was the revealed identity of Jesus as Christ and Son.

His Church is built on the revelation of who He is, not on religious tradition, denominational preference, or ministry personalities.

If the foundation is anything other than Christ revealed, the gates of Hades can and will prevail.

The Gates of Hades: Not Fire and Devils, But Unseen Realms

Jesus said the gates of Hades would not prevail against His Church. We often interpret this to mean hell, devils, and warfare. But Hades in the Greek (ᾅδης) literally means "unseen, hidden, or without light."

It is not just a place of torment; it is a realm without revelation.

Jesus was not simply talking about demons attacking the Church. He was saying:

"As long as My Church is built on revelation, the unseen realm has no authority to overthrow it."

But when churches are built on charisma, human effort, or inherited ideas, not revelation, they become susceptible to darkness. Without light, people perish. Without light, people wander. Without light, the church becomes religious, not ruling.

Preference, Personality, and Doctrinal Constructs

What we often call "church" today is built on:
- Preferences - musical styles, service lengths, fashion, or vibe
- Doctrinal constructs - theological camps and inherited biases
- Personalities - celebrity pastors and charismatic leaders

But the Church Jesus is building is not based on man-made ideologies, systems, or sentiments. It is a spiritual house, built of living stones (1 Peter 2:5), filled with glory, and governed by the King.

If we are more loyal to our denomination than to His voice,

If we are more committed to our service structure than to His presence,

If we are more concerned with crowds than with character, we are not building His Church.

False Metrics and Vain Labor

We often measure the health of a church by:

- How many people attend
- How exciting the services are
- How large the budget is
- How trendy the building looks

But Heaven measures differently:

- Is Christ being formed in the people? (Gal. 4:19)
- Are sons and daughters being raised, not just workers and volunteers?
- Is the community being transformed?
- Is the government of God increasing?
- Is truth established and revelation flowing?

Success in the Kingdom is not crowds, it's conformity to Christ.

He Builds What He Determined, Not What We Suggest

Jesus is not asking us to hand Him our blueprints. He is inviting us to receive His.

Just as Moses had to build the tabernacle "according to the pattern shown him on the mountain" (Hebrews 8:5), we must yield to divine architecture.

We must stop asking God to bless what we've built and begin agreeing with what He's already blessed.

His Church Is Not Fragile

The Church Jesus is building:

- Doesn't collapse under persecution
- Doesn't need constant reinvention
- Isn't sustained by trends or technology
- Doesn't waver in cultural storms

Why?

Because it is built on a Rock. It is anchored in revelation. It is led by the Spirit and ruled by Christ.

When man's churches fall, His Church still stands.

When denominations split, His Church still prevails.

When personalities fail, His Church still advances.

His Church is not in decline. It is indestructible.

A Call to Repent and Rebuild

This chapter is not a condemnation. It is a Kingdom confrontation, a loving call to examine the house we are building.

Are we laboring in vain, or are we yielding to the Builder?

Are we assembling crowds or raising sons?

Are we preaching ourselves or revealing Christ?

It's time to stop attending church and start becoming the Church.

It's time to dethrone personalities and enthrone the King.

It's time to re-align with His pattern and rebuild on the Rock.

Jesus is not coming back for a church that looks successful, He's coming for a glorious Church (Eph. 5:27), without spot or wrinkle, filled with Him, governed by Him, and built for Him.

This is His Church.

Reflection Questions

1. What areas of my life or ministry have I built by human effort rather than divine design?

2. How does the revelation of Christ as the foundation change my understanding of Church?

3. Have I been more committed to preference, doctrine, or personality than to revelation?

4. What might need to be torn down, in order for Christ to truly build His Church in me?

CHAPTER 2
THE EKKLESIA HE SPOKE OF

Called Out to Govern, Not Just Gather

"And I also say to you that you are Peter, and on this rock I will build My church, and the gates of Hades shall not prevail against it."
Matthew 16:18 (NKJV)

We've heard this verse countless times, but it's easy to overlook a powerful reality: Jesus never used the word "church" in the sense we understand it today. The word He used was ekklesia, and it was not a religious term.

He didn't say synagogue, temple, or priesthood. He chose a secular, governmental word and infused it with divine intention.

What Is the Ekklesia?

In ancient Greek and Roman culture, the ekklesia was a called-out legislative body, a group of citizens summoned to assemble for the purpose of governance. They debated laws, enacted policy, and represented the will of the ruling authority. They did not meet just to socialize, they met to govern on behalf of the King.

By using this term, Jesus was doing more than defining a group, He was establishing an identity and a function:

- A people called out from the world
- A people called up into heavenly authority

- A people sent forth to represent the interests of the Kingdom in the earth

The Ekklesia is not merely a place of worship, it is a governing body of Spirit-filled citizens whose assignment is to establish Heaven's rule on earth.

A Different Mandate

Most modern church structures aim to attract and retain people.

The Ekklesia, however, is called to equip and release ambassadors.

- Churches today often focus on attendance; the Ekklesia focuses on assignment.
- Churches ask, "How many came?" The Ekklesia asks, "How much authority was exercised?"
- Churches measure success by growth; the Ekklesia measures success by transformation.

When we reduce the Ekklesia to weekly events, we've already surrendered the original mandate.

Misinterpretation Through Translation

The word "church" as we use it in English is derived from the Greek word kyriakon, meaning "belonging to the Lord." That's a noble meaning, but it was not the word Jesus used.

By the time English translations emerged, the institutional church had already taken root. Over time, ekklesia was replaced by church, and instead of a people on assignment, we formed places for attendance.

This shift in language led to a shift in identity.

The Ekklesia became a building, a service, a denomination, something you go to, not something you are. This translation subtly transformed an apostolic movement into a religious institution.

From the Upper Room to the City Gates

The early Church understood what Jesus meant.

They didn't form committees, they formed communities of government.

They didn't build monuments; they became mobile tabernacles of presence and power.

They didn't wait for revival, they released Kingdom culture everywhere they went.

When persecution scattered them, the Ekklesia spread. When culture opposed them, the Ekklesia prevailed. They didn't win through might or money, they triumphed through message, maturity, and mission.

These were not just believers, they were ambassadors. And their gatherings were not just for fellowship but for alignment, equipping, and dispatching.

Ekklesia is Heaven's Embassy

An embassy is a sovereign outpost of one nation within the territory of another. It operates with the laws, authority, and culture of its home nation, even though it is geographically located elsewhere.

That's what the Ekklesia is:

A **Kingdom embassy**, an outpost of Heaven inside the earth.

- It carries Heaven's authority.
- It functions by Heaven's laws.
- It speaks Heaven's language.
- It distributes Heaven's resources.
- It enforces Heaven's agenda.

The Ekklesia does not simply sing about Heaven, it represents Heaven.

The Difference Between Church and Ekklesia

Church (as commonly practiced)	Ekklesia (as biblically intended)
Weekly religious gathering	Governing body of believers
Built around personality	Built upon revelation
Membership-driven	Mission-driven
Man-centered (consumer focus)	Christ-centered (Kingdom focus)
Seeks to fill seats	Seeks to fill cities with truth
Focused on experience	Focused on transformation

The Ekklesia is not anti-church. It is the true Church as Jesus defined it.

The Kingdom Context

You cannot separate Ekklesia from the Kingdom. To understand what the Church is, you must understand what the Kingdom is. Jesus' first and primary message was not about the Church, it was about the Kingdom:

"Repent, for the Kingdom of Heaven is at hand."
(Matt. 4:17)
"This gospel of the Kingdom shall be preached..."
(Matt. 24:14)

The Ekklesia is the vehicle through which the Kingdom is expressed.

The Kingdom is the government.

The Ekklesia is the governing assembly.

The Spirit is the power source.

And Christ is the ruling King.

This Is Why the Enemy Fears the Ekklesia

The enemy doesn't fear church services. He fears people walking in Kingdom identity and authority.

The gates of Hades cannot withstand the Ekklesia because the Ekklesia doesn't just sing, shout, and shake, it rules, binds, looses, and legislates from Heaven's perspective.

When we become the Ekklesia:

- We stop reacting to the world and start governing it.
- We stop hiding from culture and start influencing it.
- We stop surviving and start sending.
- We stop being impressed with hell and start enforcing Heaven.

Recovering the Ekklesia Mandate

We're not called to revive church culture. We're called to restore Kingdom culture through the vehicle Jesus chose, His Ekklesia.

To do that, we must:

1. Return to the revelation of Christ as King
2. Re-align our identity around our function, not just our form
3. Rebuild structures that equip people to walk in governance and glory
4. Resist the pressure to conform to popular church models
5. Refuse to trade presence for performance

A Called-Out People, Not a Called-In Crowd

Jesus is not returning for a casual congregation. He's returning for a glorious, governing Ekklesia. Not a crowd in a building, but a body in motion, called out, raised up, and sent forth.

The world doesn't need more churches. It needs more embassies of the Kingdom.

It needs people who know:
- Who they are
- Whose they are
- What authority they carry
- And why they were placed where they are

That's the Ekklesia.

That's His design.

That's our assignment.

Reflection Questions

1. What does it mean for me personally to be part of the Ekklesia, not just the Church?

2. How has the traditional model of church shaped my expectations of ministry?

3. Am I functioning more as an attendee or as a Kingdom ambassador?

4. What might shift if I saw my spiritual life as a representation of Heaven's government?

CHAPTER 3
THE REVELATION THAT BUILDS AND BINDS

The Church is built on Christ revealed, not Christ assumed.

"And I also say to you that you are Peter, and on this rock I will build My church, and the gates of Hades shall not prevail against it."
                    Matthew 16:18 (NKJV)

When Jesus declared His intention to build His Church, He didn't point to Peter's charisma, personality, or leadership potential. He pointed to what had just been revealed.

"Flesh and blood has not revealed this to you, but My Father who is in heaven."

In that moment, Jesus revealed the blueprint: His Church is not built on opinions, doctrines, or trends. It is built upon revelation, specifically the revealed identity of Christ.

Where there is no **revelation**, there is no **foundation**. And where there is no foundation, the gates of Hades can prevail.

The Rock Is Revelation

Jesus did not say, "Upon you, Peter, I will build My Church."

He said, "Upon this rock…"

What rock?

Not Peter himself, but the revelation Peter just received:

"You are the Christ, the Son of the Living God."

Revelation is not head knowledge. It is not second-hand information. Revelation is the unveiling of divine truth directly by the Spirit of God.

That's why Jesus said, *"Flesh and blood has not revealed this to you..."*

Peter did not deduce this, he received it. And the Church that Jesus builds is made of those who are not just attending but receiving truth from the Father.

What Are the Gates of Hades?

We must rethink our understanding of Jesus' next words:

"...and the gates of Hades shall not prevail against it."

We often think of this as hell, fire, warfare, and demons. But Hades (ἅδης) in Greek simply means "the unseen realm." It's not just torment, it's the absence of light, the place of no revelation.

The Church built on revelation cannot be overcome by that which lacks revelation.

Hades = Unseen, Unrevealed, Unilluminated

So, what are the "gates" of Hades?

Gates are access points. They represent entry and authority. The gates of Hades are the portals through which darkness, deception, and confusion try to enter human systems, religion, culture, education, media, and yes, even churches.

But Jesus said:

"The gates of the unseen will not prevail against what I build."

Where **revelation flows,** Hades is **powerless**.

The Tragedy of Building Without Revelation

When the Church loses revelation, it loses authority.

When it loses authority, it turns to:
- Form instead of fire
- Structure instead of Spirit
- Programs instead of presence
- Innovation instead of impartation

The result is a church that looks successful but is spiritually powerless, vulnerable to compromise, performance, and cultural erosion. We can have crowds without Christ, platforms without presence, and gifting without grounding.

The Authority of Revealed Identity

When Peter received revelation of who Jesus was, Jesus immediately turned and revealed who Peter was:

"You are Peter…"

Revelation is **reciprocal**, in this way.

You cannot know who you are until you know who He is.

This is why the Ekklesia is filled with insecure leaders, identity-confused believers, and powerless congregations, we are trying to function without revelation.

When the Church is built on personalities rather than revelation, we produce followers, not sons. When it is built on performance, we produce events, not encounters. When it is built on human vision, we produce growth, not glory.

But when the Church is built on Christ revealed, identity is unlocked, authority is released, and the unseen realm is pushed back.

From Revelation Comes Keys

"And I will give you the keys of the Kingdom..."
Matthew 16:19

The keys of the Kingdom are not given to the gifted, they are given to the revealed. God does not give keys to strangers. Keys are entrusted to sons, those who know and are known. The Church cannot function with borrowed revelation.

We must live in the flow of what the Father is revealing, not just what the last generation received.

Revelation Is Not Optional, It's Structural

Revelation is not extra, it is essential.

This means revelation is not optional or a spiritual bonus. It's not reserved for mystics, prophets, or "deep" people. It's not decoration for the spiritually elite.

Too often, people treat revelation as something extra, like a cherry on top of doctrine or tradition. But in truth, revelation is what gives life and power to truth. Without it, we are left with information but no transformation.

"It is essential"

Revelation is the very substance of how God builds. Jesus said to Peter in Matthew 16:18:

> "Upon this rock [of revelation], I will build My Church..."

This reveals that revelation is the foundation of the Ekklesia.

No revelation, no real Church.

It is the concrete, not the curtain.

The foundation, not the flair.

This is the heart of the metaphor:
- Concrete represents foundation, what the building rests on.
- Curtains represent decoration, things that hang in the house but don't hold it up.

Revelation is not ornamental, it's structural. In other words:
- Revelation is not the fancy part of the house, it's the very thing holding it together.

- You can build a house without curtains, but not without concrete.
- Many churches have spiritual "curtains" (performance, lights, charisma) but lack the solid revelation of Christ and His Kingdom.

Summary:

"Revelation is not a luxury, it's a load-bearing wall. It's not the fringe, it's the foundation. We don't accessorize the Church with revelation; we anchor it in it."

Without revelation:

- We build systems that substitute for presence
- We cling to doctrine and miss the Person
- We repeat patterns that once worked but no longer carry weight

The Ekklesia must be led by what is revealed, not by what is trending.

Revelation is timeless.
Strategy is seasonal.
And fleshly wisdom is always insufficient.

The War Is Always Over Revelation

From the beginning, Satan's strategy has been to obscure what God has said.

"Has God indeed said...?" (Genesis 3:1)

The enemy's tactic is always to confuse, twist, or conceal the voice of the Father. Why? Because where there is no revelation, there is no sonship, and without sonship, there can be no government.

The serpent fears a people who know who their Father is, who they are, and what they've been sent to do.

The Church That Prevails

The Church that prevails is the one that builds on fresh revelation of Christ.

- Not stale doctrine, but living truth
- Not man-made vision, but Heaven-born instruction
- Not secondhand information, but Spirit-breathed revelation

This Church **does not fall when culture shifts.**

This Church **does not fracture when leaders fail.**

This Church **does not fade when programs end.**

This Church is built on the Rock.

And the gates of Hades will never prevail against it.

Will You Build with Revelation or With Sand?

Jesus warned of the difference between two builders:
- One who built on sand, surface, appearance, assumption
- One who built on rock, depth, revelation, foundation

Only one house withstood the storm.

CHRISTOPHER TURNEY

Only one house stood when the flood came.

Only one house endured the shaking.

"The storm does not reveal what we built.

The storm reveals what we built on."

Reflection Questions

1. Where in my life or community have I lacked revelation and seen the gates of Hades prevail?

2. What recent truth has God revealed to me that I am building upon?

3. Have I settled for second-hand faith or am I receiving direct revelation from the Father?

4. How can I better cultivate a lifestyle of receiving fresh revelation?

CHAPTER 4
LIVELY STONES OR MAN-MADE BRICKS?

Identity is in the stone. Conformity is in the brick.

"You also, as living stones, are being built up a spiritual house..."
1 Peter 2:5 (NKJV)

"...they had brick for stone, and they had asphalt for mortar."
Genesis 11:3 (NKJV)

God always intended His house to be built with stones, not bricks. But in the plains of Shinar, men exchanged the divine for the man-made. Instead of yielding to God's design, they manufactured their own. The contrast is not just about materials, it's about mindsets and models.

One is authentic, organic, diverse, and divinely shaped. The other is uniform, accelerated, artificial, and man controlled. This is not just about Babel. This is about today's Church.

Genesis 11: A Substitute for Stone

"Then they said to one another, 'Come, let us make bricks and bake them thoroughly.' They had brick for stone, and asphalt for mortar."
Genesis 11:3

At Babel, man chose brick over stone, and asphalt over covenant mortar.

Why?

Because bricks are:

- Faster to make
- Easier to stack
- Uniform in size
- Conformist by nature
- Formed from mud and straw (earthly materials)

Bricks represent the human need to control structure, accelerate building, and produce predictable outcomes. But the moment man chose brick, he rejected divine distinction.

The Tower of Babel was man's attempt to build without God's blueprint. It was a structure of ambition, uniformity, and rebellion. And at the heart of it was a substitute material, brick for stone.

God's Pattern: Stones, Not Bricks

From Genesis to Revelation, God always builds with stones.

- He commanded altars be built with uncut stones (Exodus 20:25)
- He selected 12 stones for the memorial in the Jordan (Joshua 4)
- He chose living stones for His spiritual house (1 Peter 2:5)
- Even the chief cornerstone is Christ Himself (Ephesians 2:20)

Why stones?

Because stones are not made by man, they are formed by God.

Stones Are:

- Diverse in shape, color, and texture
- Unique in identity, no two are the same
- Heaven-crafted, not man-manipulated
- Time-tested through natural process
- Fitted together, not forced into place

God doesn't want manufactured conformity, He wants divinely hewn identity.

Bricks Demand Sameness: Stones Require Sovereignty

Bricks demand everyone look the same, fit the same, act the same. They create systems of sameness, religious clones, not Kingdom sons.

But stones cannot be forced. They must be:

- Chosen
- Prepared
- Placed with precision
- Joined by revelation, not just routine

The process takes longer. The structure emerges more slowly. But what is built is lasting, living, and filled with glory.

"God takes time because He's not building a crowd, He's building a covenant."

The Church of Bricks vs. The House of Stones

Brick-Based Church	Stone-Based Church
Uniformity and performance	Diversity and purpose
Fast growth, shallow roots	Slow formation, deep foundations
Built by men, for men	Built by God, for His glory
Formed with earthly methods	Shaped by the Spirit's leading
Dependent on control	Dependent on covenant
Prefers sameness	Honors uniqueness
Uses people as materials	Sees people as sons

We must ask: What are we building with?

Are we forming people into bricks or fitting them as stones?

The Mortar Matters

"...they had asphalt for mortar." Genesis 11:3

Asphalt, or bitumen, was tar-based and sticky, a substitute for covenant.

It reflects systems held together by:

- Performance
- Pressure
- Preference
- Programs

But God's structure is held together by covenant and Spirit-led alignment, not by manipulation or artificial adhesives.

In man's systems, people are stuck together.

In God's house, people are joined together.

Jointly Fit Together

"...in whom the whole building, being fitted together, grows into a holy temple in the Lord."
                                                            Ephesians 2:21

Stones must be fitted, not stacked.

This takes time.

You can't just put any stone next to another. You have to wait for the one that fits.

And that's the beauty of God's process:

He doesn't force us to conform, He places us where we fit.

This is why identity is essential in the Ekklesia. If we don't know who we are, we'll settle for being whatever we're shaped into, even a brick.

Babel's Message vs. Zion's Mandate

At Babel, man said:

> *"Come, let us build ourselves a city... lest we be scattered abroad..."*   (Genesis 11:4)

It was about:
- Name
- Control
- Centralization

But at Zion, God says:

"You are a chosen generation, a royal priesthood... living stones..." (1 Peter 2:9–10)

It is about:

- Identity
- Calling
- Glory

One structure is for man's glory, the other is for God's habitation.

The Return to Stonework

This is a prophetic call to return to the stonework of the Spirit.

- To embrace God's shaping over man's shortcut
- To honor the uniqueness of every living stone
- To allow the Lord to place people where they fit, not where they fill a role
- To break the cycle of religious brickmaking
- To build altars, not towers

The world is tired of brick churches, high-reaching, soul-draining, artificial constructs. It's time for living, breathing, joined-together places of presence. The Church Jesus is building doesn't rise quickly. It rises intentionally, stone by stone, glory by glory.

Let the Stones Speak

Even Jesus said:

"If these should keep silent, the stones would immediately cry out." (Luke 19:40)

The stones still have a voice. Each one has a testimony. Each one is part of the architecture of His glory.

You are not a brick.

You are not mass-produced.

You are not here by chance.

You are a living stone, chosen, shaped, and placed by the Master Builder.

Ambition to Reach Heaven Instead of Colonize Earth

At the heart of the Babel project was an ambition to ascend, not to obey.

"Come, let us build ourselves a city, and a tower whose top is in the heavens; let us make a name for ourselves..."
Genesis 11:4)

They were not trying to bring Heaven down; they were trying to go up. Their goal was not dominion in the earth but escape from it.

In this, we see a reflection of many modern churches:

- Programs built around getting people out of here, rather than preparing them to reign here
- Ministries obsessed with arrival (heaven), rather than assignment (earth)
- Gospel messages centered on evacuation, rather than occupation

They were building a man-made system to reach God, rather than stewarding what God gave them dominion over.

"God never told us to build a ladder to Heaven. He told us to bring His Kingdom to earth."

Fear of Judgment, Not Faith in Promise

Some scholars suggest that the Tower of Babel was more than rebellion, it was a reaction to fear. Even after God promised not to flood the earth again, they didn't believe Him.

So they said in effect:

"If another flood comes, this tower will save us."

In other words:

- Let's build our own salvation.
- Let's insulate ourselves from judgment.
- Let's create a system that bypasses repentance and trust.

This mirrors modern churches that build religious structures to guard themselves from God, rather than yield to Him in covenant.

They construct programs, performance, and platforms as a shield against intimacy and accountability.

Instead of faith in His promise, they build mechanisms to avoid His presence.

Disunity as Divine Intervention?

When man builds apart from God, God confounds the language.

He interrupts the unity of ambition to preserve the purity of assignment.

"But the Lord came down... and confused their language, that they may not understand one another's speech."
(Genesis 11:5–7)

Could it be that some church disunity is not just demonic, but divine disruption?

Could it be that:

- God is disrupting ambition?
- God is dismantling false unity that's built on image, not identity?
- God is preventing systems from ascending in pride instead of remaining in purpose?

Where ambition seeks to climb, God confounds.

Where covenant seeks to obey, God collaborates.

Return to Dominion, Not Departure

God's mandate has never changed:

"Be fruitful, multiply, fill the earth, subdue it, and have dominion..." (Genesis 1:28)

This was not a mandate to leave, it was a mandate to transform. The true Ekklesia does not dream of leaving the earth, it exists to fill it with glory. We are not building ministries to escape judgment, but to release justice. We are not creating towers to reach Heaven, but houses where Heaven rests on earth.

The Babel model says:

"Let's go up."

The Kingdom model says:

"Let it come down."

Reflection Questions

1. Have I allowed myself to become a 'brick' rather than a 'stone' in God's house?

2. Am I valuing speed and uniformity over uniqueness and divine placement?

3. Where am I trying to ascend rather than steward what God gave me to colonize?

4. How can I better honor others as stones God is shaping for His purpose?

CHAPTER 5
THE GOVERNMENT OF THE KINGDOM

The Ekklesia was never meant to be managed, it was meant to govern.

"For unto us a Child is born, unto us a Son is given; and the government will be upon His shoulder."
                                    Isaiah 9:6 (NKJV)

"Of the increase of His government and peace there will be no end..."
                                    Isaiah 9:7

The Ekklesia that Jesus is building is more than a spiritual family or a worship center. It is a governmental agency, an extension of Heaven's dominion into the earth. It is the Ekklesia, a called-out assembly authorized to enforce the rulings of the King.

Too many have viewed Church as a hospital, a harbor, or a stage. While it may bring healing, safety, and inspiration, that is not its core function.

The true Ekklesia is a governmental embassy. It does not operate on democracy, preference, or emotion, but by divine appointment, prophetic clarity, and Kingdom constitution.

Government Rests on the Son

Isaiah's prophecy makes something stunningly clear:

"The government will be upon His shoulder."

Not His head, His shoulder. Why?

Because the shoulder represents the Body. Christ is the Head, and we, His Ekklesia, are the Body through which He expresses and executes His government in the earth.

This means that Kingdom government flows through the Ekklesia, not separate from it. And not just any church, but the one that is rightly joined to the Head, rightly aligned in function, and rightly submitted to the Spirit.

What Is Government in the Kingdom?

Government is not control, it is order, structure, and authority under the King's rule.

In the natural, government defines:

- Boundaries
- Laws
- Enforcement
- Citizenship
- Resource distribution

Likewise, in the Kingdom, government ensures:

- Alignment with Heaven's will
- Proper order in spiritual function
- Guarding and advancing territory
- Righteous judgment and justice

The Ekklesia is not just a worshipping body, it is a governing council with legislative authority in the Spirit.

Apostolic Government and Divine Order

In 1 Corinthians 12:28, Paul outlines God's order in the Church:

"And God has appointed these in the church: first apostles, second prophets, third teachers..."

This is not about status, it's about structure. God establishes an order through which His government flows. Apostles and prophets are not celebrities, they are foundation layers and architects (Eph. 2:20).

This order is designed to:

- Equip the saints
- Establish doctrine
- Ensure spiritual alignment
- Advance the Kingdom

Without apostolic and prophetic government, the Church becomes an institution led by popular vote, personal vision, or inherited structure rather than divine authority.

Jesus Gave Keys to Govern

"I will give you the keys of the Kingdom of Heaven..."
(Matt. 16:19)

Keys represent access, authority, and administration. They are not decorative, they are functional. Jesus didn't give us microphones; He gave us keys. Not for performance, but for governing access points.

What are these keys for?

- Binding and loosing (legislative authority)
- Unlocking understanding (revelation)
- Opening gates for Kingdom entry (salvation, healing, deliverance)
- Closing doors to darkness (intercession, decree, spiritual resistance)

To have keys is to have jurisdiction, and the Ekklesia is called to operate in jurisdictional authority over regions, cities, and nations.

From Pastors Only to Kingdom Governance

The Church has often been led solely by pastoral models, shepherds who care, comfort, and counsel. This is essential, but it's only one part of the governmental structure.

Without apostolic and prophetic dimensions, the church becomes:

- Maintenance-minded instead of mission-driven
- Survival-oriented instead of territorially advancing
- Comfort-centered instead of Kingdom-carrying

Pastors gather. Apostles govern. Teachers explain. Prophets expose and align. Evangelists harvest. The Ekklesia hosts and legislates.

The full function of Christ's government requires the fivefold gifts functioning in unity and maturity (Eph. 4:11–13).

Heaven Needs Alignment to Act

"Your Kingdom come, Your will be done on earth as it is in heaven." Matthew 6:10

This is not just a prayer, it's a protocol.

The Ekklesia's role is to align earth with Heaven. To do so, we must be:

- Submitted to His authority
- In sync with His timing
- Speaking what Heaven is saying

Heaven doesn't move through **ambition**, but through **alignment**. And government in the Kingdom is never about control, it's about representation.

Church Without Government Is Powerless

When there is no structure, we have chaos. When there is no government, we have noise but no authority. Just as in civil society, disorder in the Church results in:

- Confusion of voices
- Competing agendas
- Doctrinal instability
- Immaturity and drift

The Ekklesia is called to be a pillar and ground of the truth (1 Tim. 3:15), not just a place for fellowship, but a house that establishes what is true, just, and aligned.

Occupy Until He Comes

"Do business (occupy) until I come." (Luke 19:13)

Jesus did not say "Wait around" or "Hold revival services" until He comes. He said "Occupy", take territory, steward influence, enforce My government. The Ekklesia is not waiting for escape, it is managing the Kingdom on earth until the King returns.

To occupy means:

- To rule with humility
- To administer resources with justice
- To influence culture without compromise
- To protect regions from darkness through spiritual legislation

We are not the bystanders of the age. We are ambassadors of a Kingdom with orders from the Throne.

The Increase of His Government

Isaiah 9:7 declares:

> *"Of the increase of His government and peace there will be no end."*

God's government is not shrinking, it's increasing. And He increases it through us.

Through every:

- Righteous decision
- Kingdom-minded leader
- Apostolically aligned church

- Son or daughter walking in identity and authority

The Ekklesia expands the government of God—not by politics, but by presence, not by force, but by faithfulness.

The Church That Governs Will Not Be Shaken

In Hebrews 12:28, we are told that we are receiving a Kingdom that cannot be shaken. That Kingdom comes with government.

The Church that is governed by Heaven:
- Can withstand cultural shaking
- Can navigate political chaos
- Can protect regions from spiritual infiltration
- Can release Heaven's economy, justice, and mercy

"A governed Church is a grounded Church. And a grounded Church is a growing Church."

This is what the Ekklesia was always meant to be, Heaven's government in the earth.

Reflection Questions

1. Do I view the Church as a place of comfort or as a center of governance?

2. How can I better align with the governmental structure of the Kingdom?

3. Am I walking in Kingdom authority or still waiting for permission to act?

4. What area of influence has God called me to occupy until He comes?

CHAPTER 6
EMBASSIES OF HEAVEN IN THE EARTH

The Ekklesia is not just a meeting, it's a manifestation of another realm.

"Now then, we are ambassadors for Christ..."
2 Corinthians 5:20 (NKJV)

"Your Kingdom come, Your will be done on earth as it is in heaven."
Matthew 6:10

Jesus taught us to pray something radical: not that we would escape to Heaven, but that Heaven would come here. The Ekklesia is the mechanism through which that prayer becomes reality.

We are not just believers; we are representatives of a greater government. We are not merely attendees; we are delegates sent to enforce the will of the King. And where we gather in His name, that space becomes Kingdom territory, an embassy of Heaven.

What Is an Embassy?

An embassy is a sovereign territory of one nation that exists within another.

It is:

- Governed by the laws of its homeland
- Staffed by representatives of the sending nation
- Protected by the authority of the ruler it represents

- Not under the jurisdiction of the host nation

When the Ekklesia gathers, we are not merely "having church" we are operating as a spiritual embassy, governed by the laws, culture, and resources of Heaven even while surrounded by the world.

"Wherever the Ekklesia is rightly functioning, the Kingdom is present."

Ambassadors, Not Just Members

Paul said, *"We are ambassadors for Christ..."* (2 Corinthians 5:20).

Not entertainers. Not event planners. Not Sunday-only spectators. Ambassadors.

Ambassadors:

- Represent the interests of the King
- Speak only what they've been authorized to say
- Operate with diplomatic immunity in hostile territory
- Are stationed in foreign lands but never disconnected from home government
- Are trained, sent, and protected by the sending nation

We are not from here. We are sent here.

The Church is not trying to survive the world, it is sent to influence it with Kingdom truth.

The Legal Authority of the Ekklesia

In Roman culture (the setting of Jesus' day), the term ekklesia referred to a governing council of citizens authorized to carry out the edicts of Caesar in occupied regions.

Jesus redeemed that word and showed us:

"My Ekklesia will not advance Rome's rule, it will release Mine."

This means the Ekklesia:

- Enforces Heaven's justice
- Declares the King's decrees
- Judges between truth and error
- Looses what Heaven looses, and binds what Heaven binds (Matthew 16:19)
- Exerts spiritual jurisdiction over the region it is assigned to

A true Ekklesia is legal territory of Heaven, and it does not function by the permission of the world, but by the mandate of the Throne.

Culture Carriers, Not Culture Chasers

Too many churches today chase relevance by mirroring the culture they were called to change. But the Ekklesia is called to carry Heaven's culture, not mimic man's.

We are a nation within a nation, and we operate under:

- A different economy (Philippians 4:19)
- A different language (faith and truth)

- A different value system (honor, humility, holiness)
- A different priority (seek first the Kingdom)

The Church was never meant to become "seeker-friendly" by diluting identity. It was called to become Kingdom-authentic, so that the earth could taste Heaven.

Wherever the Ekklesia is, there should be:

- Righteousness established
- Healing flowing
- Truth declared
- The poor lifted
- Sons and daughters rising
- Demonic strongholds losing their grip

That's what an embassy does: it extends its nation's influence.

The Embassy Is Not the Destination, It's the Deployment Center

In natural terms, embassies are not where you move to live, they are where you go to:

- Be trained
- Be protected
- Be resourced
- Be sent

Likewise, the Ekklesia is not a place to hide from the world.

It's the sending station of Heaven, a training ground for sons, a throne room for prayer, and a launching pad for assignment.

We gather to be:

- Refreshed in identity
- Recalibrated in vision
- Refueled by grace
- Released with authority

"The goal is not just attendance, it's deployment. Not just filling seats but filling cities. Not just growing a church but growing the Kingdom."

Embassies Function in Hostile Territory

Embassies are not welcomed by all, especially in hostile nations. Yet they remain untouched, because:

- They are protected by their home government
- They answer only to the authority of their King
- Any attack on them is considered an attack on the nation they represent

This is true of the Ekklesia. We are in the world, but we are not of it. We are in enemy-occupied territory, but we are not subject to it.

We are protected by the:

- Blood of the Lamb
- Word of the King
- Power of the Spirit
- Favor of Heaven's host

When we function as Heaven's embassy, no weapon formed against us can prosper (Isaiah 54:17).

The Embassy Carries Heaven's Provision

Embassies are fully funded by the government that sends them. They do not rely on the economy of the land they are in. They are resourced by the nation they come from.

Likewise, the Ekklesia is funded by Heaven.

We do not depend on:
- The systems of man
- The donations of the crowd
- The opinions of the wealthy

We depend on:
- Kingdom provision
- Covenant blessing
- Supernatural resource flow

Our provision is tied to our position, when we are rightly aligned, the windows of Heaven are open.

Heaven Is Looking for Ground to Land On

"On earth as it is in Heaven."

God is not looking for performances, He is looking for places of alignment.

Places where Heaven can touch earth.

Places where the King is obeyed.

Places where the Kingdom is made visible. Wherever the Ekklesia is gathered in revelation and authority, Heaven has a landing strip.

When we walk in that kind of alignment:

- Miracles become normal
- Revelation becomes fresh
- Cities are changed
- Nations are discipled

We Are His Embassy, And We Carry His Name

"Go therefore and make disciples of all the nations…"
(Matthew 28:19)

The Great Commission is not just about converts, it's about nations. We are called to establish embassies in every territory. Not just buildings, but bases of Kingdom culture. Not just services, but stations of transformation.

The Church was never meant to be one global denomination. It was always meant to be a global network of embassies, each one unique, but united by the same Constitution, Spirit, and King.

Let the Embassy Arise

We must shift from:

- Church attendance to Kingdom representation
- Spectator Christianity to ambassadorial living
- Event-driven gatherings to embassy-level impact

You are not just a church member.

You are an ambassador.

You carry Heaven.

You speak for the King.

And where you stand, the Kingdom stands with you. Let every house of worship become an embassy of authority. Let every gathering become a dispatch center for sons and daughters. Let every believer rise, not as a visitor in the earth, but as an authorized representative of Heaven.

Reflection Questions

1. In what ways does my life reflect the authority of an ambassador?

2. Is the place I worship functioning like a Kingdom embassy?

3. Am I properly connected to Heaven's government or operating independently?

4. What can I do to represent Heaven's economy, language, and values more clearly?

CHAPTER 7
THE CULTURE OF THE KINGDOM

The Ekklesia does not mirror culture, it manifests it.

"You are a chosen generation, a royal priesthood, a holy nation, His own special people, that you may proclaim the praises of Him who called you out of darkness into His marvelous light."
1 Peter 2:9 (NKJV)

Culture is not just what you say, it's how you live. It's the invisible atmosphere that shapes thinking, behavior, priorities, and values.

Every kingdom has a culture.

And the Kingdom of God is no exception.

If the Ekklesia is Heaven's embassy, then the Kingdom is its culture. That means the Church is not just called to preach the Kingdom, we are called to embody it.

Culture Is Heaven's Signature on Earth

The goal of the Church is not to "fit in" to the surrounding culture. It is to model a higher way of living that reflects Heaven's order.

Culture includes:
- Language (how we speak)
- Economy (how we give and receive)
- Relationships (how we love and honor)

- Time and values (what we prioritize)
- Behavior and customs (how we live daily life)

Jesus didn't come to start a religion. He came to introduce a government with a distinct culture that could be seen, heard, tasted, and touched.

"The Kingdom of God is not eating and drinking, but righteousness, peace, and joy in the Holy Spirit."
(Romans 14:17)

Culture vs. Counterfeit

Much of modern church life has adopted cultural trends from the world, marketing tactics, entertainment formats, and business models.

But these are substitutes for the culture of the Kingdom, which is formed through:

- Surrender, not strategy
- Holiness, not hype
- Honor, not hierarchy
- Glory, not glamour

When the Church adopts the world's methods to reach the world, we often end up producing a worldly church rather than a holy Ekklesia.

Culture isn't changed by imitation; it's changed by infiltration.

The Culture of Heaven Is the Character of Christ

To manifest the culture of the Kingdom, the Ekklesia must reflect the nature of the King.

The Ekklesia is not about:

- Having a good time, but producing good fruit
- Having inspiring services, but creating a Kingdom atmosphere
- Having flashy gifts, but raising mature sons and daughters

Culture is built around:

- Character over charisma
- Fruit over fame
- Obedience over optics

Heaven's Language: Truth and Honor

Every culture has a language. The language of the Kingdom is not gossip, flattery, or fear. It is:

- Truth spoken in love
- Honor for all people (1 Peter 2:17)
- Declarations aligned with God's Word

The Ekklesia must speak differently than the world:

- Not echoing the news cycle, but prophesying Heaven's report
- Not reacting in fear, but responding in faith
- Not cursing darkness, but proclaiming light

Heaven's Economy: Generosity and Supply

Kingdom culture includes an economy, but not based on scarcity.

It's built on:
- Seed and harvest
- Giving and receiving
- Tithes, offerings, and supernatural provision

In the Kingdom:
- We give to grow
- We sow to unlock cycles of abundance
- We live to bless, not to store up

The Ekklesia must model a culture of generosity, not pressure or guilt, because generosity flows from maturity, not manipulation.

Heaven's Values: Humility, Holiness, and Honor

Heaven doesn't value popularity, it values purity. It doesn't prioritize crowds; it prioritizes conformity to Christ.

Kingdom values include:
- Humility as the pathway to exaltation (James 4:10)
- Holiness as normal, not rare (1 Peter 1:16)
- Honor as a climate that makes room for glory (Matthew 13:57–58)

The Ekklesia does not chase what the world prizes, we embody what the King loves.

Atmosphere: The Culture of Presence

In many churches today, there is atmosphere, but not presence. There is energy, but no glory. There is movement, but no weight. Kingdom culture is a glory atmosphere, tangible evidence that God is in the midst.

It includes:

- Stillness that honors God
- Order that flows from the Spirit
- Spontaneity anchored in truth
- Worship that reveals, not just entertains

Wherever the Ekklesia gathers, the climate should shift.

Customs of the Kingdom

Just like every culture has customs, the Kingdom has its own:

- Laying on of hands (Acts 13:3)
- Breaking bread together (Acts 2:42)
- Tithing and offerings (Hebrews 7:8)
- Baptism and communion (Acts 2:38; 1 Cor. 11:26)
- Prophesying, declaring, decreeing (1 Cor. 14:3; Job 22:28)

These are not religious traditions; they are cultural markers of the government we belong to.

The Culture We Carry Determines the Kingdom We Release

You cannot preach what you do not embody.

You cannot export what you have not cultivated.

If we claim to be an embassy of Heaven but carry a culture of:
- Offense
- Competition
- Control
- Performance

…then we are not truly Ekklesia.

Culture isn't something we adopt, it's who we become by abiding in Him.

"As He is, so are we in this world." (1 John 4:17)

Culture Change Requires Reformation, Not Revival

Revival awakens the dead.

Reformation realigns the awakened.

The Ekklesia is not a company of the dead, but those which are alive in Christ!

The Ekklesia must be willing to confront false cultures:
- Celebrity Christianity
- Entertaining church experiences
- Shallow discipleship
- Consumerism in worship

We must tear down Babel towers of man-made culture and rebuild with stones of Kingdom identity.

Culture Preaches Louder Than Sermons

People will forget your message, but they won't forget how your culture made them feel.

- Culture teaches people how to behave
- Culture establishes the boundaries of what's acceptable
- Culture determines whether people grow or shrink, thrive or hide

The Ekklesia must intentionally shape Kingdom culture in everything:

- How we greet one another
- How we correct one another
- How we steward time
- How we celebrate diversity

Heaven's Culture, On Earth, Through Us

Jesus didn't say *"On earth as it is in Heaven"* to give us poetry.

He gave us permission.

He gave us a model, not just for prayer, but for culture:

- Forgiveness
- Honor
- Unity
- Worship
- Authority
- Joy
- Righteousness

The Ekklesia is Heaven's model home, built to display the culture of a Kingdom not of this world.

Reflection Questions

1. What culture does my spiritual community carry, Kingdom or worldly?

2. How does my speech reflect the language of Heaven?

3. Do I carry an atmosphere of righteousness, peace, and joy?

4. How can I intentionally cultivate Kingdom culture in my home, church, or workplace?

CHAPTER 8
THE CALL TO DISCIPLESHIP

The Ekklesia raises sons, not spectators.

"Go therefore and make disciples of all the nations..."
Matthew 28:19 (NKJV)

"Until Christ is formed in you..."
Galatians 4:19

Discipleship is not a program. It's not a course. It's not even a class. Discipleship is the **process of transformation,** where **identity is shaped, character is forged,** and **Kingdom culture is transferred into sons and daughters.**

In the true Ekklesia, people don't just "attend." They are **trained, fathered,** and **formed**.

From Members to Disciples

Church membership has often replaced discipleship. But Jesus never said, *"Make members."* He said, *"Make disciples."*

Church Membership	Kingdom Discipleship
Join a community	Surrender to a process
Sign up for benefits	Lay down your life
Remain as you are	Be transformed into His image
Attendance-based	Assignment-based
Passive participation	Active engagement
Comfort-focused	Christ-focused

Membership gives you a seat. Discipleship gives you identity, discipline, and authority.

The Goal Is Formation, Not Retention

Paul's cry was not to keep people in a system, it was:

"My little children, for whom I labor in birth again until Christ is formed in you…" (Gal. 4:19)

This is the cry of true apostles and shepherds, not to impress people, but to form Christ in them.

Understanding discipleship:

- Discipleship isn't about behavior modification. It's about identity transformation.
- It doesn't make better churchgoers. It forms mature Kingdom sons.
- It doesn't rush to performance. It patiently establishes rootedness and fruitfulness.

Discipleship Happens in the Context of Family and Government

Discipleship doesn't happen in isolation. It happens in relational alignment, inside the culture of the Ekklesia.

That culture includes:

- Fathering voices that speak identity and correction
- Prophetic alignment that exposes error and calls people higher
- Apostolic structure that builds people from the foundation up

- Real community where vulnerability, accountability, and transformation are normal

You cannot disciple people you're trying to impress. You cannot disciple people you're afraid to correct.

You cannot disciple people without revealing your scars and your strength.

The Pattern of Discipleship Is Jesus

Jesus didn't disciple the masses. He discipled a few. And those few turned the world upside down.

His pattern?

- Walk with Me (relationship)
- Learn from Me (instruction)
- Obey what I command (application)
- Be sent in My name (delegation)

He wasn't raising servants; He was raising sons who would walk in His authority. He didn't cater to comfort, He called people to follow, leave, surrender, and die daily.

Discipleship Is Costly

Jesus said:

"If anyone desires to come after Me, let him deny himself, take up his cross, and follow Me." (Luke 9:23)

The Ekklesia must recover the cross as the starting point of discipleship, not just an altar call, but a lifestyle. Why? Because the cross is where, who we thought we were dies, and who He made us to be lives.

Discipleship calls people:

- From independence to obedience
- From entitlement to honor
- From emotion to endurance
- From gifts to fruit
- From crowds to the cross

It's not cheap grace. It's Kingdom grace, which empowers surrender, not self-preservation.

The Fivefold Functions Equip Disciples

Ephesians 4:11–13 makes clear that apostles, prophets, evangelists, pastors, and teachers exist:

"...for the equipping of the saints for the work of ministry, for the edifying of the body of Christ..."

Discipleship is not the pastor's job alone.

It is the assignment of the whole governmental structure of the Ekklesia.

- Apostles lay foundations and send
- Prophets expose lies and realign identity
- Teachers equip through instruction and doctrine
- Pastors shepherd the soul and tend wounds
- Evangelists awaken faith and invite obedience

Each gift plays a role in the discipleship of the saints, not to keep them busy, but to bring them into maturity and mission.

From Consumers to Contributors

Church culture often teaches people to consume:
- "Get fed"
- "Be blessed"
- "Receive your breakthrough"

But the Ekklesia calls people to contribute:
- "Take up your cross"
- "Be sent"
- "Make disciples"

Disciples don't just attend, they build, give, serve, pray, fast, teach, and multiply. They don't just listen, they lean in.

True Discipleship Produces Reproduction

The sign of discipleship is not how much you know, it's how much you multiply. Jesus told His disciples:

"Go and make disciples..." (Matt. 28:19)

You are not truly discipled until you are:
- Discipling others
- Raising sons and daughters
- Transferring what you've received

The goal is not spiritual dependency.

The goal is Kingdom deployment.

The Ekklesia Disciples Nations, Not Just Individuals

Jesus didn't say, "Disciple people." He said, "Disciple nations."

That means the Ekklesia must:

- Think regionally, not just relationally
- Disciple systems, education, economy, government, media
- Equip leaders in every sphere, not just the pulpit
- Form Kingdom-minded believers who influence culture from the inside

The Church is not a daycare, it's a discipleship engine to shift nations.

It's Time to Build Again

We've had enough:

- Inspirational messages without formation
- Services without surrender
- Gifts without growth
- Crowds without crosses

It's time to build people again. It's time to recover the fire of intentional, costly, covenantal discipleship. The Ekklesia exists not to host events but to form sons. Not to entertain but to establish. Not to grow platforms but to grow people.

Reflection Questions

1. Am I being discipled or just attending church?

2. What areas of my life need deeper formation and surrender?

3. Who am I actively discipling and raising in the Kingdom?

4. How can I grow from spiritual consumer to Kingdom contributor?

CHAPTER 9
SONSHIP, THE MATURITY OF THE HOUSE

"You are no longer a servant, but a son… and if a son, then an heir through Christ". Galatians 4:7

The Ekklesia is not a business. It's not a performance center. It's not a religious factory. It is a house, and in every house, maturity is measured not by attendance or activity but by sonship. God is not trying to grow a religious crowd; He's raising sons and daughters.

This is the maturity of the house.

From Orphanhood to Ownership

Paul writes:

"As long as the heir is a child, he differs nothing from a servant, though he is lord of all…" (Galatians 4:1)

Immaturity keeps sons functioning like servants. And many churches are full of believers who love God but still live like orphans:

- Striving for approval
- Competing for affection
- Performing for position
- Operating out of insecurity and fear

The Ekklesia exists to break the orphan spirit and restore people to identity, inheritance, and intimacy.

The House Is Governed by Sons, Not Slaves

When Moses built the house under the Law, it was a servant's house.

But when Jesus came:

"Christ as a Son over His own house, whose house we are..." (Hebrews 3:6)

The new house is governed by sons, not slaves.

This means:

- We serve, but out of love, not obligation
- We obey, but from identity, not insecurity
- We honor, because it's in our nature, not out of fear
- We grow, not just in knowledge, but in likeness to our Father

The house functions at the level of sonship it raises. When the Church stays in servanthood, it builds systems. When it steps into sonship, it builds legacy.

Sonship Is the Pattern of the Kingdom

The Kingdom doesn't advance by crowds, it advances by sons.

"Unto us a Son is given... and the government will be upon His shoulder." (Isaiah 9:6)

Everything God does in the earth; He does through sons:

- The earth groans for the manifestation of the sons of God (Romans 8:19)

- The Son (Jesus) brings many sons to glory (Hebrews 2:10)
- The Father gave authority to the Son and through Him to us (John 5:22; Luke 10:19)

Jesus is not just the Savior, He is the pattern Son, showing us what it means to walk as a son in the house.

Servants Work. Sons Build

Servants do what they are told. Sons carry the Father's heart.

In the Ekklesia:

- Servants focus on tasks; sons focus on transformation
- Servants come for a paycheck; sons come to build legacy
- Servants seek reward; sons seek inheritance

Jesus said:

"A servant does not abide in the house forever, but a son abides forever." (John 8:35)

This is why performance culture must die in the Church. We're not training volunteers, we're forming sons.

This concept has been a fundamental principle of operation here at Kingdom Reign Ministries. We do not solicit volunteers for service, to fill the void departmentally. We have focused on raising sons in the house that will "Be led by the Spirit" regarding their service.

This creates an obedience in service, not obligation to fill a need. This approach requires a willingness for an organic development of people and can only be accomplished by a patience, and greater concern for character development than department development. Now **sons are stewarding**, not just **serving**!

Sons Carry Responsibility, Not Just Authority

Authority flows through sonship, but with it comes responsibility.

Sons:

- Protect the atmosphere of the house
- Confront what threatens the family
- Discern the heart of the Father
- Walk in alignment, not independence
- Prepare to inherit, not just receive

Mature sons don't just serve, they steward. The Ekklesia must shift from shallow empowerment to deep formation. Gifts may attract people, but only sonship forms the foundation that holds weight.

The House Needs Fathers and Sons

Paul writes:

"Though you have ten thousand instructors in Christ, you do not have many fathers…" (1 Corinthians 4:15)

The Church is full of teachers but lacking true fathers.

Fathers:
- Impart identity
- Shape character
- Transfer inheritance
- Provide discipline and covering

Sons:
- Receive correction
- Carry responsibility
- Honor the pattern
- Multiply what's been entrusted

The maturity of the Ekklesia is directly connected to the restoration of father-son order.

Maturity Is Measured by Sonship, Not Activity

How do you know a house is maturing? Not by how many services it hosts. Not by how trendy the music is. Not even by how gifted the leaders are.

You know it's maturing when:
- People stop **competing** and start **covering**
- Worship is about **presence**, not **performance**
- Correction is received as **love**, not **rejection**
- **Assignment** takes **priority** over **preference**
- Sons are being **sent**, not just **kept**

The Ekklesia is a sending house, not a storage room. Sons are not trophies, they are arrows (Psalm 127:4–5), and they are sent to take territory.

The Earth Groans for Sons

Creation is not groaning for another church service. It's groaning for sons to take their place.

"For the earnest expectation of the creation eagerly waits for the revealing of the sons of God."
(Romans 8:19)

Sons don't hide in the church. They reign in the earth. They carry the image of the Father into business, government, education, the arts, and the nations.

The Ekklesia exists to:

- Raise them
- Equip them
- Send them
- Cover them

This is the maturity of the house.

When the House Is Full of Sons…

When the Church becomes a house of sons:

- Offense dies
- Loyalty rises
- Legacy is possible
- Inheritance is safe
- Honor is instinctive
- Glory finds a resting place

A church full of servants may grow fast, but a house of sons will last.

This is the maturity Christ is after. Not a church filled with gifted strangers, but a family of formed sons.

Reflection Questions

1. Am I functioning as a son or as a servant in the house of God?

2. Do I know who my spiritual fathers are—and am I receiving from them?

3. Where have I resisted correction instead of receiving it as a son?

4. How can I help create an environment that raises mature sons and daughters?

CHAPTER 10
JOINTLY FIT, THE ARCHITECTURE OF THE BODY

The Church is not a crowd; it's a construction.

"...from whom the whole body, joined and knit together by what every joint supplies, according to the effective working by which every part does its share, causes growth of the body..."
Ephesians 4:16 (NKJV)

"You also, as living stones, are being built up a spiritual house..."
1 Peter 2:5

The Ekklesia is not random. It is not a spiritual flash mob. It is a God-architected structure, fitted stone by stone, member by member, and joint by joint. It is an intentional design, built not on preference but on placement.

This is not a scattered people.

This is a jointly fit body, a divine blueprint of covenantal connection, mutual supply, and Kingdom alignment.

God Never Builds with Isolation

The world celebrates independence. But the Kingdom builds through interdependence.

The Ekklesia is described as:

- A Body (1 Cor. 12)

- A House (1 Pet. 2:5)
- A Temple (Eph. 2:21)
- A City (Matt. 5:14)
- A Bride (Rev. 21:2)

Every one of these metaphors emphasizes connection, nothing stands alone. We were never meant to grow in isolation. Every part is important. Every connection is vital. You don't get built because you believe, you get built when you are joined.

Jointed, Not Just Gathered

Ephesians 4:16 says the body grows *"by what every joint supplies."*

Joints are where parts connect. And supply doesn't come just from your gift, it comes through your alignment.

- You can have a great calling and still be ineffective if you're not joined.
- You can be gifted but stagnant because you're unsubmitted.
- You can love God but still leak because you're not rightly connected.

God doesn't anoint loose parts. He anoints fitted ones.

Placement Is God's Prerogative

"But now God has set the members, each one of them, in the body just as He pleased." (1 Cor. 12:18)

You don't place yourself in the body. You don't get to pick your position based on comfort or preference. God places you where you are most needed, not just where it's convenient.

When we reject God's placement, we:

- Disconnect from supply
- Disrupt the blueprint
- Dishonor the body
- Delay maturity

The Kingdom does not operate like the world. In God's house, the architect places the parts, and sons honor the design.

Paul writes in 1 Corinthians 12:28, *"And God hath **set** some in the church, first apostles, secondarily prophets, thirdly teachers..."* The word translated "set" is the Greek word tithēmi, which means to place, to appoint, to lay down as a foundation, to ordain, to establish in a fixed position.

This word reveals intentionality. God does not scatter His people randomly into the body; He strategically positions them according to His eternal design. Just as the stones of Solomon's temple were cut and prepared to fit without sound of hammer or chisel on site (1 Kings 6:7), so God has already prepared and "set" His people into their precise place in the Ekklesia.

To be "set" means:

- Foundation, not accident – It implies blueprint language, as when a cornerstone is laid and every other stone aligns from it.
- Permanence, not trial-and-error – God's setting is not experimental or provisional; it is deliberate and enduring.

- Function, not favoritism – Placement is not about status but about purpose. Apostles are "first" not in superiority but in sequence, because divine order requires foundation before framework.

When Paul emphasizes that "God set," he removes human prerogative. Men may appoint, elect, or hire, but only God can "set." His setting determines structure, flow, and authority. To resist His placement is to resist His architecture.

The significance is this: the Ekklesia is not built by human innovation but by divine blueprint. God alone has the prerogative of placement, because only He sees the whole design. Our role is not to choose our place but to faithfully occupy it.

Every Part Has a Supply

"...by what every joint supplies..."

You carry something the house needs. And the house carries something you need. There are no spare parts in the Kingdom.

There are no spectators in the Ekklesia.

- Your word matters.
- Your prayer matters.
- Your presence matters.
- Your obedience matters.
- Your placement matters.

God doesn't waste material. If He set you in the body, you carry supply.

Disconnection Diminishes Supply

You can have power and still leak. When we're not rightly aligned:

- Strength drains
- Discernment dulls
- Fire fades
- Gifting feels empty
- Purpose becomes foggy

Disconnected believers don't realize they've cut off their own oxygen. And disconnected churches lose their authority because God doesn't approve ambition, He approves alignment.

If we're going to build something that lasts, we must stop chasing "fit in" and start walking in "jointly fit."

Unity Is Not Sameness, It's Fit

God isn't building with bricks (uniform, man-made). He's building with stones, each one unique, but fit together.

"...fitly framed together..." (Ephesians 2:21)

Unity is not everyone looking or acting the same. It's every part functioning where it was designed and valuing the placement of the others.

The enemy hates fit because:

- Fit brings strength
- Fit releases flow
- Fit protects the blueprint
- Fit produces fruit

The Cost of Misfit

When people move themselves out of place:

- The house weakens
- The rhythm is disrupted
- The flow is broken
- Others must overcompensate for what was lost

When churches reject apostolic "fit" for institutional comfort, they trade:

- Power for performance
- Glory for growth metrics
- Formation for flattery

Misalignment is not neutral, it's dangerous.

There Is a Stone That Fits Where You Are

In true apostolic building, we don't just need people, we need the **right ones** in the **right place**. Just like stones in a wall, each placement must:

- **Complement** what's next to it
- Be **shaped to match** its moment
- **Wait until** the time and **placement is right**

God doesn't just send people to a church. He **sets them in place**. Some stones are shaped in the field. Others are chiseled in private. But when the time is right, they are **fit into the house with purpose**.

Jointed for Growth and Glory

"...causes growth of the body for the edifying of itself in love." (Ephesians 4:16)

Growth isn't caused by ambition. It's caused by joints. By **honor**. By **humility**. By **obedience**. By **divine fit**.

The Church grows when:

- People are planted
- Gifts are activated
- Order is honored
- The Spirit is welcomed
- The blueprint is obeyed

Every joint, every ligament, every part doing its share causes growth.

The Blueprint Demands a Fit

We cannot build His house with our preferences. We must build with His pattern. This is not about recruiting volunteers. This is about discerning fit, protecting unity, and advancing together.

The days of **disconnected** Christianity are over.

The hour of the **jointly fit** Church has come.

This is how the structure rises. This is how the glory comes. This is how we hold weight. This is how the Ekklesia stands.

Reflection Questions

1. Am I truly joined to the Body or simply nearby?

2. What supply do I carry, and am I releasing it?

3. Where am I called to be fit in this season of building?

4. Who are the people I am rightly aligned with, and how can I strengthen those joints?

CHAPTER 11
THE GLORY IN THE HOUSE, THE OBJECTIVE

"...and the glory of the Lord filled the house of God."
2 Chronicles 5:14 (NKJV)

"The latter glory of this house shall be greater than the former..." Haggai 2:9 (ESV)

The Ekklesia is not complete when it gathers. It is not complete when it grows. **It is complete when it becomes a dwelling place for glory**. Glory is the objective of all that is built. Glory is not a side effect; it is the **destination of divine order**.

God never instructed man to build something that He would not inhabit. The glory is not a reward. It is the **proof of Heaven's endorsement**.

Glory Is Not Hype, It Is Weight

The Hebrew word for glory is kavod, which means:

- Weight
- Substance
- Heaviness of honor and presence

Glory is not a feeling. It is not atmosphere alone. It is divine evidence, the substance of God Himself.

When the glory of God fills a house:

- Man cannot minister

- Flesh is silenced
- Sin is exposed
- Healing flows
- Worship erupts
- Holiness becomes natural

Glory is the environment of Heaven, and it is the goal of the Ekklesia on earth.

Order Precedes Glory

"And when the priests came out of the Holy Place… the house, the house of the Lord, was filled with a cloud."
(2 Chronicles 5:13–14)

In Solomon's temple, the glory did not fill the house until the order was complete:

- The ark was in place
- The priests were consecrated
- The Levites were in position
- The singers were unified
- The song was *"He is good, and His mercy endures forever"*

Then, and only then, did the cloud of glory fill the house so powerfully that no one could stand to minister.

"Glory does not rest on disorder.
Glory responds to alignment, holiness, and honor"

The Ekklesia must recover the fear of the Lord, or we will entertain crowds but never host glory.

The Pattern Always Leads to the Presence

Every time God gave a blueprint, whether for the tabernacle, the temple, or the New Covenant Church, it was for the same reason:

"Let them make Me a sanctuary, that I may dwell among them." (Exodus 25:8)

God has always desired to dwell, not just to visit. He desires a resting place, not a revolving door. The blueprint was not about impressing people. It was about creating a place that could hold the weight of His presence.

The Glory Comes to Houses, Not Just Individuals

Personal encounters are powerful. But corporate glory is what transforms regions.

When the house is:

- Built rightly
- Governed justly
- Aligned deeply
- Consecrated fully

…glory can rest there.

God is not just looking for spiritual individuals, He is looking for a spiritual house.

Ichabod Is the Warning of a Gloryless House

"The glory has departed from Israel…" (1 Samuel 4:21)

Ichabod was the name given when the ark of God was captured, and the presence was lost.

Churches that:
- Abandon the Word
- Resist the Spirit
- Reject alignment
- Substitute performance for presence risk becoming Ichabod houses: busy, beautiful, even well-funded, but gloryless.

What we need is not more events, it's more evidence of Heaven. The Ekklesia is meant to host Him, not just talk about Him.

The Latter House Shall Be Greater

"The glory of this latter house shall be greater than the former..." (Haggai 2:9)

This is not nostalgia for Solomon's temple. It is a prophecy about us, the corporate Ekklesia, made of living stones, filled with the Spirit.

The glory of the New Covenant house:
- Is not in a building, but in the Body
- Is not limited to one location, but spreads like leaven through regions
- Is not seasonal, it is increasing and eternal

The latter house is not just bigger, it's better. Because it's built on the Cornerstone of Christ, inhabited by sons, and designed for fullness, not fragments.

When Glory Fills the House...

When the glory fills the Ekklesia:

- The priesthood becomes powerful
- The Word becomes fire
- The atmosphere becomes holy
- Worship becomes revelation
- Walls fall and hearts burn

We no longer minister to people, we minister to the Lord. And from that glory, the nations are transformed.

The Church That Hosts the Glory Must Be Willing to Surrender

You cannot carry glory and cling to:

- Control
- Compromise
- Carnality
- Competition

Glory sanctifies, clarifies, and terrifies the flesh.

It demands:

- Holiness over hype
- Covenant over crowds
- Fire over familiarity

God will not place His glory on something we refuse to yield.

Glory Is the Objective, Everything Else Is Decoration

Programs are helpful. Structures are needed. Gifts are beautiful. Teams are essential. But without glory, it's all just religious decoration.

God's presence is not a luxury, it's the point. It's why we gather. It's what we long for. It's what separates us from every other gathering in the world. The Ekklesia is not a performance hall. It is a holy habitation.

Prepare the House, Invite the Glory

If we build it His way, He will fill it. If we honor the pattern, He will inhabit it. If we humble ourselves, He will lift us in His presence. Let every Ekklesia pray like Moses:

"If Your Presence does not go with us, do not bring us up from here." (Exodus 33:15)

Let every church rise to become:

- A house of sons
- A house of prayer
- A house of alignment
- A house of glory

Because that's the objective. He must dwell.

Reflection Questions

1. Have I prioritized glory, or substituted it with hype or growth?

2. What would it look like for my life or church to be a resting place for God's glory?

3. Is there anything in my house (life or ministry) that must be cleansed for the glory to come?

4. Am I willing to let go of personal agendas to host the presence of God fully?

CHAPTER 12
THE PROPHETIC BLUEPRINT BUILDING ACCORDING TO HEAVEN'S PATTERN

If Heaven didn't draw it, don't build it.

"See that you make all things according to the pattern shown you on the mountain."
Hebrews 8:5 (NKJV)

"Unless the Lord builds the house, they labor in vain who build it." Psalm 127:1

There is a divine pattern in Heaven for what God desires in the earth. And the call of the apostolic Church, the Ekklesia, is to build what God has revealed, not what man has imagined.

The Ekklesia is not a copy of the culture. It is the construction of a Kingdom. Not built by hype or tradition, but by prophetic revelation and apostolic architecture. God is not looking for innovation without instruction. He's looking for people who will say:

"I will only build what You have shown."

Every Manifested plan of God Begins with a Blueprint

From the tabernacle of Moses to the temple of Solomon...

From the blueprints of Noah's ark to the measurements in Ezekiel's vision...

From the formation of the early Church to the unfolding design in Revelation...

God always reveals a pattern before He releases His presence.

And that pattern is:

- Specific
- Spirit-given
- Weighty
- Non-negotiable

You do not get to "wing it" and expect glory.

You build according to the blueprint, or you labor in vain.

Moses on the Mountain: The Original Apostolic Model

"Make everything according to the pattern shown to you on the mountain." (Exodus 25:9)

Moses did not download ideas from culture. He ascended the mountain, received the pattern, and built the tabernacle to Heaven's specification.

This is apostolic building:

- It begins with ascension, entering the place of revelation
- It receives instruction, clarity on function and design
- It manifests glory, because it mirrors what exists in Heaven

The tabernacle Moses built wasn't man's creation. It was Heaven's replication.

David's Dream, Solomon's Construction

David had the vision. Solomon built the structure. But neither moved without a pattern.

"All this," David said, "the Lord made me understand in writing by His hand upon me, all the works of these plans." (1 Chronicles 28:19)

Prophetic building is not guessing. It is revealed, written, and obeyed. Solomon's temple became a dwelling place for glory because it was constructed from Heaven's pattern, not personal preference.

Jesus: The Builder of a Different Kind of House

"I will build My Church..." (Matthew 16:18)

Jesus never said He would build a temple, synagogue, or structure of stone. He said He would build an Ekklesia, a governing body of called-out sons built on the rock of revelation.

Every piece of this house is:

- Chosen
- Placed
- Aligned
- Purposed

The true Church isn't grown through marketing strategies. It's built through prophetic blueprint and **apostolic foundation.**

Paul the Master Builder

"According to the grace of God given to me, as a wise master builder I have laid the foundation..." (1 Cor. 3:10)

Paul didn't just plant churches, he built according to a divine architectural plan.

He laid:

- Foundations of doctrine
- Structures of leadership
- Alignments of order and gifting
- Systems of discipleship and sonship

He warned:

"Let each one take heed how he builds..." (1 Cor. 3:10)

Why? Because God's house must be built with fear, wisdom, and revelation.

Heaven Has a Pattern for the Ekklesia Today

Heaven is still speaking. And God is still revealing blueprints for what His house must look like:

- A house of prayer
- A house of glory
- A house of sons
- A house of government
- A house of alignment
- A house of legacy

He is revealing designs for:

- Regional hubs
- Training centers
- Spiritual families
- Kingdom communities
- Kingdom economies

But we must ascend, see, and submit to what He shows.

Beware of Manmade Blueprints

Many are building today:

- Ministries without mission
- Churches without government
- Programs without power
- Movements without maturity

They are building crowds, brands, buildings, but not necessarily the Church Jesus is building. Just because it works doesn't mean it's Kingdom. Just because it grows doesn't mean it's authorized.

If it's not built from Heaven's pattern, it may attract people but repel glory.

The Blueprint Protects the Glory

The reason for the pattern is not restriction, it's protection.

When we build His way:

- His presence can dwell without being defiled
- His people are aligned for inheritance
- His purposes are not delayed

- His glory finds a place to rest

The pattern is the container for the weight of Heaven. And when we follow it, we don't just grow, we go from glory to glory.

A Call to the Builders

If you are a pastor, leader, planter, apostle, prophet, teacher, this chapter is for you. Heaven is calling you back to the mountain of revelation.

Do not build from memory.

Do not build from someone else's model.

Do not build to impress men.

Build from what you see in Him.

Let your cry be:

> "Show me the pattern."
> "I will not move without the blueprint."
> "I will not labor in vain."
> "I will build according to Your design."

Legacy Requires Deliberate Forecasted Vision

If we want the next generation to carry glory, they must be raised in houses that are:
- Built by revelation
- Anchored in identity
- Governed with righteousness

- Filled with sons and daughters
- Aligned with Heaven's voice

The blueprint we build by today is the foundation they will inherit tomorrow.

Build What Heaven Has Authored

This is the mandate of the Ekklesia:

- Not to mimic, but to model
- Not to experiment, but to establish
- Not to compete, but to construct according to Heaven's decree

We are not entertainers. We are builders. We are not inventors. We are carriers of the pattern revealed from the Throne.

"Unless the Lord builds the house, they labor in vain who build it."   Psalm 127:1

Let us rise as wise master builders. Let us construct houses fit for sons, flames, and glory. Let us receive the pattern and build it with joy. This is the Ekklesia. This is Heaven's embassy in the earth. This is the blueprint of God.

Reflection Questions

1. Am I building what Heaven has shown or what man has modeled?

2. When was the last time I received a clear pattern from the Lord, and have I obeyed it?

3. What structures in my ministry or thinking need to be aligned with Heaven's blueprint?

4. How can I become more sensitive to receive, steward, and build from divine revelation?

CHAPTER 13
THE ORDER OF ESTABLISHMENT RECLAIMING DIVINE CHRONOLOGY

"And God has set some in the church, first apostles, second prophets, third teachers, after that miracles, then gifts of healings, helps, governments, diversities of tongues."
1 Corinthians 12:28 (KJV)

The modern church has become obsessed with retention, keeping people, filling seats, and sustaining interest. In the name of "engagement," we build programs to pacify dysfunction instead of building people into divine alignment.

We put hurting people into positions, hoping that involvement will create transformation. But service does not heal wounds, truth does. Programs do not produce purpose, God's order does. And the longer we keep bypassing God's divine sequence, the more we perpetuate instability.

God Has a Chronology, Not a Hierarchy

1 Corinthians 12:28 does not list ministry functions by importance, but by order, chronology. It is not about status; it is about sequence. When we reverse or ignore this order, we interrupt what God intends to manifest in the house.

Let's break it down:

1. First apostles
2. Second prophets
3. Third teachers
4. After that... miracles

5. Then... gifts of healings
6. Helps
7. Governments
8. Diversities of tongues

Apostles and Prophets in the Ekklesia

Those who argue that apostles and prophets no longer exist in the modern church are, in a sense, correct, because the modern religious system called "church" is not the same as the Ekklesia Jesus is building. God did not set apostles and prophets into denominational boards, Sunday services, or humanly-constructed organizations. He set them in His Ekklesia.

That distinction is critical. The church men have built may not have room for apostles and prophets but the Ekklesia God builds cannot exist without them. Paul says plainly: "God hath set some in the church, first apostles, secondarily prophets..." (1 Cor. 12:28). To deny their existence is to either:

1. Admit that what is being built is not the Ekklesia at all,
2. Or confess that man's version of "church" has chosen to operate outside of God's blueprint.

Apostles and prophets are not optional features; they are foundational elements (Eph. 2:20). Without them, what stands is not God's building but man's substitute. This is why placement is His prerogative: only the Builder Himself can decide which stones form the foundation, which are structural supports, and which complete the framework.

So yes, apostles and prophets may be absent from churches, but they remain essential in the Ekklesia. Their existence is not tied to man's acceptance but to God's eternal setting.

This is a divine blueprint for establishing the Church, and it reveals something staggering:

If the Church wants sustained miracles and effective helps, it must establish the preceding order first.

You can't jump to "helps" when the house has no apostolic foundation. You can't activate "healing" among those who are still being fragmented by false teaching. You can't experience "governments" when the prophets have been silenced and the apostles dishonored.

Programs Are Not the Problem, Substitutions Are

We are not attacking structure or scheduling. Order, discipleship systems, and care ministries have their place. But when programs replace presence, and roles replace relationship, we end up with function without foundation.

Churches are often filled with hurting people helping hurting people, and burnout is inevitable. But 1 Corinthians 12:28 reveals that "helps" comes after healing, not before.

- Helps is not therapy.
- It is ministry born out of wholeness.

We are plugging people into service to keep them from leaving, instead of equipping them for purpose. And when there are no true apostles or prophets setting order, the result is spiritual codependency disguised as community.

Where Are the Pastors and Evangelists?

You may ask: *"Where are pastors and evangelists in this list?"*

Here is the revelation:

- They are not omitted; they are simply functioning in different places.
- Pastors tend to the flock, in pastures, homes, hospitals, and highways.
- Evangelists gather the harvest, outside the walls, in streets and cities.

They are vital to the mission of the Church. But when we place them in governmental roles inside the house, they often operate outside their grace, leading to fatigue, burnout, and frustrated sheep.

"God has set...", Apostles, prophets, and teachers are the ones set in the house for order, doctrine, and spiritual government.

All five gifts, apostles, prophets, evangelists, pastors, and teachers are for the equipping of the saints (Ephesians 4:11–12). But not all five are governmental in the same way within the ekklesia.

Reformation Requires Re-identification

The Body of Christ is undergoing a great reformation, and part of that process is re-identifying function.

We must:

- Restore apostles and prophets to foundational roles.
- Recommission teachers to ground the house in truth.
- Release pastors and evangelists to operate in their fields.
- Stop assigning broken people to roles that require healing.
- End the performance-based cycle of plugging people into ministry to stop them from leaving.

This isn't **exclusion**. This is **divine positioning.**

When we follow His chronology, we experience:

- Order → Presence
- Revelation → Miracles
- Identity → Wholeness
- Government → Growth
- Healing → Helps

Why Programs Alone Aren't Working

We're building ministries that sustain people's interest but not their identity. We're developing leadership tracks that train hands but not hearts. And it's because we're skipping the "first things." We want "after that" results without "first" order.

Until we restore the apostles to the foundation, the prophets to the blueprint, and the teachers to the structure we will continue to patch with programs what can only be healed by alignment.

Chronology Unlocks Glory

This is not legalism. This is not elitism. This is divine construction. God builds His house in order, not in haste.

If we want:

- Miracles to last
- Healing to flow
- Helps to be sustainable
- Government to be righteous

…then we must get the first things first.

"God has set some in the church, first…"

That's not man's idea. That's Heaven's instruction.

We Must Return to His Pattern

- Not just to grow churches, but to build people.
- Not just to keep people, but to heal them.
- Not just to fill pulpits, but to establish altars.

This is what it means to be His Ekklesia.

Not a reactionary institution, but a governmental house, built by divine chronology and sustained by glory.

Reflection Questions

1. Have I elevated church programs above God's divine order?

2. Am I placing people into ministry roles who haven't been healed or discipled?

3. Do I understand the distinct roles of apostles, prophets, teachers, pastors, and evangelists in the Church?

4. What must be re-ordered in my life or ministry to honor 1 Corinthians 12:28?

CHAPTER 14
THE INVISIBLE FOUNDATION, THE UNSEEN NECESSITY OF APOSTLES AND PROPHETS

"Having been built on the foundation of the apostles and prophets, Jesus Christ Himself being the chief cornerstone..." Ephesians 2:20 (NKJV*)*

When God builds, He begins with foundations, not platforms. Not what is visible to the crowd, but what is weight-bearing, alignment-setting, and almost entirely unseen.

Apostles and prophets are not flashy personalities or celebrity voices. They are invisible graces, set in place to carry the weight of heaven's construction.

Foundations Are Not Highlights, They're Hidden

In a world obsessed with platforms, God is still looking for foundations. We elevate visibility. He values invisibility. We crave popularity. He builds with humility. Apostles and prophets are not the attractive part of the structure. They are the essential part. They are not the windows that bring light, or the walls that people see. They are the hidden bedrock of the building.

They don't want to be seen. They must be felt, in alignment, integrity, strength, and continuity.

Their Grace Is Weight-Bearing

A true apostolic or prophetic grace is not cosmetic, it is constructive. It doesn't decorate, it lays alignment. It doesn't entertain, it carries burden. It doesn't seek notice, it creates structure.

Their presence makes the rest of the building possible. Their absence makes the building vulnerable and collapsible.

Jesus Is the Cornerstone, Not the Platform

The only part of the foundation meant to be seen is the Cornerstone, Jesus.

- The apostle connects us to Him.
- The prophet aligns us with Him.
- The teacher expounds Him.
- The Church reflects Him.

But if the cornerstone is not aligned, the whole building is off. And if the foundational graces are absent or self-centered, the alignment cannot last. The role of apostles and prophets is not to shine, but to submit to the Cornerstone.

Why Many Churches Feel Weak

The Church becomes powerless when:

- Apostles are replaced by administrators.
- Prophets are silenced or sensationalized.
- Foundations are substituted with programs.
- The Cornerstone is replaced with personalities.

We feel the instability, the shifting values, the shallow roots. We feel the performance pressure to build quickly with bricks instead of stones. But it is only through the unseen foundation that the Church becomes what she is meant to be, immovable, enduring, and glorious.

The Cost of Being Foundational

Apostolic and prophetic ministry is not for the faint of heart. It requires:

- Being misunderstood, because your work is underground.
- Being overlooked, because your gift is not ornamental.
- Being immovable, because everything rests on you.
- Being sacrificial, because the weight is not evenly distributed.

If God uses you to be part of the foundation, don't expect applause. Expect pressure.

This is why Paul said, "God has exhibited us apostles last, as men condemned to death" (1 Corinthians 4:9).

To be foundational is to die beneath the thing you help build. And yet, there is no higher honor.

They Are Felt, Not Flaunted

You don't walk into a building and compliment the foundation. But you feel it in the stability, the peace, the strength of the structure.

In the same way:

- Apostolic grace brings governmental peace.
- Prophetic grace brings revelatory clarity.
- Together, they create a space where the Church can grow in safety and alignment.

They are not the face of the Church, Jesus is. They are not the center of the house, He is. But without them, His fullness has no foundation to dwell upon.

They Must Be Recovered

Many churches are floundering because they've tried to skip the unseen parts. You can't build with bricks and expect the strength of stones. You can't fill positions and ignore foundations.

It's time to recover:

- Apostles who father movements, not manage brands.
- Prophets who reveal the blueprint, not chase platforms.
- Foundations that carry, not compete.

We cannot build for glory without laying what is weight-bearing. And we cannot host God's presence in a house that cannot hold its own structure.

The Most Necessary Parts Are the Least Seen

Paul wrote, *"Those members of the body which seem to be weaker are necessary"* (1 Corinthians 12:22).

That's true of the Body. It's also true of the House. The most necessary parts are often the least celebrated. But they are God-chosen, Christ-connected, and grace-fitted. And when they are rightly laid, Heaven has something to dwell in.

Reflection Questions

1. Have I been seeking visibility instead of becoming foundational?

2. How can I grow in apostolic or prophetic grace without craving spotlight?

3. Is my ministry building on a foundation aligned to the Cornerstone, or on something else?

4. What parts of the Church am I called to carry, even if no one sees me doing it?

CHAPTER 15
THE SOUND OF THE HOUSE, PRESENCE, ALIGNMENT, AND GOVERNMENTAL WORSHIP

"Indeed it came to pass, when the trumpeters and singers were as one... the house of the Lord was filled with a cloud."
2 Chronicles 5:13–14 (NKJV)

"But at midnight Paul and Silas were praying and singing hymns to God... and suddenly there was a great earthquake, so that the foundations of the prison were shaken..."
Acts 16:25–26 (NKJV)

Every house has a sound. Every move of God carries a frequency, an audible expression of what He is doing and saying. And every Ekklesia must recover its sound from heaven, not from culture.

Sound is More Than Music, It Is Atmosphere

Sound is not entertainment. It's atmosphere-setting.

The sound of the house establishes:
- Atmosphere for the glory of God
- Alignment of the people under one voice
- Authority in the realm of the spirit

The Church was never meant to be a venue for performances or personality-driven worship. It was meant to be a dwelling place of presence, a space where Heaven touches earth through unified sound.

When Sound Aligns, Glory Comes

In 2 Chronicles 5, the trumpeters and singers became one sound, and the house was filled with glory to such a degree that no one could stand.

There was no striving. No prompting. No emotional hype.

There was only:
- Unity
- Obedience
- Sound

This wasn't just musical excellence. It was spiritual alignment. Glory doesn't come because we sing louder, it comes when we become one. When the sound matches the blueprint, the house is filled.

Worship is the God Centered Adoration that Frees Us

In Acts 16, Paul and Silas were not just praising, they were **governing**. Bound in chains, surrounded by prisoners, they raised a sound that shook the foundations of their bondage.

That's the sound of the Ekklesia:
- Not victimized praise, but victorious proclamation
- Not reactive worship, but governmental declaration

Their worship was not a coping mechanism, it was an act of alignment that forced the prison to respond.

We Must Discern the Sound of the House

Not every sound belongs in the house. Some sounds are:

- Manufactured
- Entertaining
- Cultural
- Empty

But the sound of the Ekklesia must be:

- Spirit-birthed
- Presence-driven
- Aligned with Heaven
- Christ-exalting

It is not about preference, genre, or trend, it's about hosting the voice of the Lord.

Recovering the Sound of Zion

Psalm 137 records the heartbreak of exiles who hung their harps and wept by Babylon's River.

"How shall we sing the Lord's song in a foreign land?"
(Psalm 137:4)

Zion's sound was not welcome in Babylon, and neither is the sound of the Kingdom welcome in carnal religious systems.

But God is calling us to:

- Take down the harps
- Return to worship
- Release a Zion sound, a sound of identity, government, and sonship.

The Sound Reveals the DNA of the House

You can tell what a house values by what it sounds like.

- Is there a sound of hunger, or entertainment?
- A sound of worship, or self-focus?
- A sound of groaning intercession, or polished performance?

The Ekklesia doesn't mimic the marketplace. It doesn't echo Egypt. It releases Heaven's sound into the earth.

Minstrels, Psalmists, and Prophetic Song

The restoration of true worship involves the restoration of function:

- Minstrels shift the atmosphere (see 2 Kings 3:15)
- Psalmists sing what God is saying (Psalm 45:1)
- Levites minister to the Lord (Ezekiel 44:15–16)

God is raising up a new priesthood of sound carriers, those who don't just sing to the room but sing from the throne. They don't release a set list; they release a scroll.

The Government is in the Sound

God doesn't just ride on notes, He rides on agreement. That's why He *"inhabits the praises of His people"* (Psalm 22:3).

True praise invites His presence. True presence releases His governmental authority. Where there is a pure sound, aligned to Heaven, bondages break and structures shake.

What's the Sound of Your House?

Not the song selection, but the spiritual atmosphere. Not what you hear with ears, but what Heaven recognizes.

The Ekklesia must rediscover its sound of glory, a sound that welcomes the King, shifts the room, and builds the house.

Reflection Questions

1. What kind of sound is my house producing, performance or presence?

2. Are we more focused on musical excellence than spiritual alignment?

3. How can our worship invite not just emotion, but authority and breakthrough?

4. What steps can we take to recover the "sound of Zion" in our local Ekklesia?

CHAPTER 16
LEGACY AND GENERATIONS
BUILDING BEYOND OUR DAY

"They shall rebuild the old ruins, raise up the former desolations, and repair the ruined cities, the desolations of many generations." Isaiah 61:4 (NKJV)

"For David, after he had served the purpose of God in his own generation, fell asleep..." Acts 13:36 (ESV)

God's dream has never been limited to one generation. His vision spans lineage, legacy, and inheritance. While many are building for attendance, God is raising houses that build for generations.

The Ekklesia Is a Multi-Generational House

The true Church is never built on the charisma of one leader or the passion of one era. It's built to outlive its builders.

- Abraham looked for a city beyond his lifetime.
- David gathered resources for a temple he'd never enter.
- Paul trained Timothy and Titus to carry the work onward.

The Ekklesia is **apostolic in mission** and **generational in structure**.

Legacy Is Not What You Leave Behind, It's Who

We often think legacy is a list of accomplishments or a succession plan. But in the Kingdom, legacy is people. Legacy is not what you do, it's who you raise.

- Sons and daughters carry the sound of the house.
- Fathers and mothers shape the culture of the future.
- Generations multiply the grace embedded in a house.

We're Not Called to Finish It; We're Called to Build It Right

Hebrews 11 tells us the heroes of faith died in faith, not having received the promise. They didn't fail, they built rightly, and trusted God to bring the increase in the appointed time.

This is why:

- Moses trained Joshua.
- Elijah mentored Elisha.
- Jesus commissioned disciples.
- Paul fathered sons.

Each generation must hand the tools to the next, sharpened by wisdom, anchored in truth, and full of power.

Apostolic Houses Build for the Future

The apostolic does not just restore, it builds beyond.

- It doesn't just preserve heritage, it prepares inheritance.
- It doesn't just guard truth, it entrusts it to faithful men (2 Timothy 2:2).
- It doesn't just teach, it fathers.

Apostolic houses refuse to waste energy maintaining the crowd. They pour into sons, daughters, and disciples who will carry the Kingdom forward.

Fathers Build What They May Never See

David's greatest act was not slaying Goliath, it was preparing for Solomon to build the temple. He drew the blueprint. He gathered gold. He instructed his son. And he let go. That is legacy, building for someone else to finish.

The Curse Is Broken Through Generational Continuity

Malachi 4:6 says that God will turn the hearts of fathers to children, and children to fathers, lest He strike the earth with a curse.

This implies:

- Disconnection breeds dysfunction
- Isolation invites destruction
- Legacy is God's design to break generational decay

When a house is rooted in legacy, the curse of fatherlessness is broken, and the blessing of continuity flows.

You're Not Just Building a Church, You're Raising a Bloodline

The Ekklesia is a spiritual family, not a weekend show.

- We're not raising members. We're raising heirs.
- We're not planting events. We're planting inheritance.
- We're not protecting attendance. We're transferring authority.

This is the cry of the Ekklesia:

> *"May the sons and daughters of this house go farther, faster, and deeper in God than we ever dreamed."*

What Will Outlive You?

Your sermon might be forgotten. Your building might fall. Your style will fade.

But what you impart into people, especially sons and daughters, lives on.

- Build what lasts.
- Pour into the next.
- Leave a living legacy.

Because the true test of a house is not its present crowd, but its future fruit.

Reflection Questions

1. Am I building for now, or for what comes after me?

2. Who am I raising to carry the mantle, message, and mission of the house?

3. Have I embraced my role as a spiritual father, mother, son, or daughter?

4. What systems, structures, or relationships need to be shaped for legacy?

CHAPTER 17
NOT A COMMUNITY CHURCH

The word ekklesia was never intended to mean "a community church." That phrase, though widely accepted and often well-meaning, is a subtle but significant downgrade of the Church's divine mandate. The Ekklesia is not called to serve the community in the way modern culture defines service.

It is not a volunteer center. It is not a program hub. It is not a social club tailored to meet the preferences, demands, or comfort zones of the surrounding population. It is a spiritual embassy of the Kingdom of God, positioned to serve the Lord amid the community and influence entire regions through divine order and apostolic governance.

"As they ministered to the Lord and fasted, the Holy Ghost said..." (Acts 13:2)

Even in its worship, the Ekklesia is first ministering unto the Lord, not the people. And it is from this posture of devotion and alignment that true apostolic commissioning and regional assignment emerge.

Called to the Lord, Planted in the Earth

The priesthood of the Ekklesia mirrors the pattern of the Levites: they were not assigned to serve the people first; they were chosen to serve the Lord. Only by serving Him faithfully were they able to bring life to the camp. Likewise, the Ekklesia is called to host God's presence, proclaim His word, and demonstrate His

Kingdom, not accommodate the shifting demands of a community-oriented consumer culture.

When a church begins designing its gatherings and ministries around what the community wants instead of what the Kingdom requires, it has already shifted its foundation. Kingdom culture is not built on consensus or survey. It is built on revelation and obedience.

The Danger of Becoming Community-Driven

While compassion and outreach are vital, the moment a church seeks approval from the region it was meant to confront and transform, it loses its edge. A regional principality is never overthrown by a church that seeks to be liked more than it seeks to be aligned. Too many churches have traded their assignment for acceptance, becoming chaplains of the region instead of ambassadors of Christ.

The Ekklesia is not called to mirror the community, it is called to reform it.

> *"You are the salt of the earth... You are the light of the world..."* (Matthew 5:13–14)

Light does not conform to darkness. Salt does not taste like what it preserves. Likewise, the Church must not be indistinguishable from the region it is called to reach.

Ekklesia: A Regional Government, Not a Local Preference

The original Greek term ekklesia referred to a governing assembly summoned to legislate and determine matters of culture, policy, and societal direction. In the Kingdom context, the Ekklesia represents Heaven's government manifested on earth, not a local church reacting to neighborhood trends.

The Ekklesia is designed to impact regions, not just run programs.

> *"Paul... went through Syria and Cilicia, strengthening the churches."* (Acts 15:41)

Apostles were not sent just to churches; they were sent to territories. They understood that the Lord's desire was not just to grow gatherings but to establish government, His government, in the spiritual and cultural climate of entire cities and regions.

When Service Is Unto the Lord, Influence Is in the Region

Modern church culture often asks, *"How can we serve our community better?"* While well-intentioned, that question must be reframed: *"How can we serve the Lord more faithfully in the midst of our community?"*

The answer to regional transformation is not simply relevance, it is reverence. When the Ekklesia serves the Lord, He releases strategy to impact cities. This is how Paul could enter regions steeped in idolatry, witchcraft, and pagan worship and emerge with Kingdom outposts of truth, power, and discipleship.

The early Church turned the world upside down not because it blended in, but because it brought Heaven's rule into earth's rebellion.

Apostles Are Sent to Territories

Apostles are not just sent to "churches", they are sent to regions to establish God's order and raise sons in every territory. The Ekklesia is the framework for this apostolic blueprint.

> *"I left you in Crete that you might set in order what was lacking..."* (Titus 1:5)

Paul left Titus not merely to grow a local church, but to establish order across the region. The same apostolic impulse is needed today. God is not looking for trendy churches in every town—He is raising apostolic and prophetic houses that carry a regional mandate, operate in spiritual government, and influence the atmosphere of entire territories.

Conclusion

The Ekklesia was never meant to be a mirror of the community, it was always meant to be the voice of the Kingdom in the region. The shift from "community church" to "Kingdom embassy" is not a matter of branding; it is a matter of assignment. The Church that Jesus is building will not be molded by the people around it, but by the word from Heaven within it.

Let the Ekklesia rise, not to please communities but to represent the King.

Reflection Questions

1. In what ways has the modern Church drifted into serving the community's preferences instead of God's purposes?
2. How can a local church remain compassionate and engaged without compromising its Kingdom identity?
3. Why is it important to distinguish between regional influence and local popularity in apostolic ministry?
4. What adjustments can your ministry or church make to ensure it is serving the Lord in the community rather than serving the community?

About the Author

Apostle Christopher K. Turney is the founder and apostolic leader of Kingdom Reign Ministries, a global ministry dedicated to proclaiming and demonstrating the gospel of the Kingdom. With over four decades of ministry experience, he has traveled extensively, teaching, preaching, and equipping leaders, churches, and believers to walk in Kingdom authority, sonship, and purpose.

Known for his revelatory insight and ability to unfold Scripture with clarity and depth, Apostle Turney's message consistently calls the Church to return to Christ's original design: the manifestation of His Kingdom on earth. His teaching emphasizes the culture, government, and economy of the Kingdom, helping believers break free from religious tradition and embrace their full inheritance as sons and daughters of God.

In addition to Ekklesia, Chris is the author of multiple books, including 'Called to Sonship', 'Kingdom Wealth', 'They Shall Be Saved', 'We Wrestle Not', 'Tithing: Law or Liberty', and 'Unashamed: From Shame to Sonship'. Each work carries his passion for grounding truth in the Word of God while calling readers to walk it out in everyday life.

Chris resides with his wife Jill, in the United States and continues to serve the Body of Christ through writing, teaching, and mentoring, raising up leaders who will carry the message of the Kingdom to the nations. He continues to travel and speak at conferences, seminars, and local churches.

CHRISTOPHER TURNEY

For speaking invitations or ministry inquiries:

Email: chris@krmchurch.com

Mailing: 4550 NE Palmetto Dr.

Jensen Beach, Florida 34957

Web: www.chrisandjillturney.com

www.ingramcontent.com/pod-product-compliance
Lightning Source LLC
Chambersburg PA
CBHW071212160426
43196CB00011B/2268